3 9082 0620509 W9-BZG-464

CHANG

B

ROYAL OAK PUBLIC LIBRARY
222 E. ELEVEN MILE ROAD
P.O. BOX 494
ROYAL OAK, MI 48068-0494

DEMCO

Change Your Child's Behavior by Changing Yours

13 New Tricks to Get Kids to Cooperate

BARBARA CHERNOFSKY
AND
DIANE GAGE

PUBLIC LIBRARY

JUL 25 1996

ROYAL OAK, MICH.

649.64
C
c1

CROWN TRADE PAPERBACKS/NEW YORK

*To all of the parents I have worked with who motivated
me to "put it in a book."*
B.C.

To Kevin, my inspiration.
D.G.

Copyright © 1996 by Barbara Chernofsky and Diane Gage

All rights reserved. No part of this book may be reproduced or transmitted in any
form or by any means, electronic or mechanical, including photocopying,
recording, or by any information storage and retrieval system, without permission
in writing from the publisher.

Published by Crown Trade Paperbacks, 201 East 50th Street, New York, New
York 10022. Member of the Crown Publishing Group.

Random House, Inc. New York, Toronto, London, Sydney, Auckland

CROWN TRADE PAPERBACKS and colophon are trademarks of Crown
Publishers, Inc.

Printed in the United States of America

Design by Barbara Balch

Library of Congress Cataloging-in-Publication Data
Chernofsky, Barbara.
    Change your child's behavior by changing yours: 13 new tricks to get kids to
cooperate/ Barbara Chernofsky and Diane Gage.—1st pbk. ed.
        p.   cm.
    Includes bibliographical references.
    1. Parent and child—Handbooks, manuals, etc.   2. Parenting—
Handbooks, manuals, etc.   3. Child rearing—Handbooks, manuals, etc.
I. Gage, Diane.   II. Title.
HQ755.85 C495   1996
649'.64—dc20   95-24089
                                                                                  CIP

ISBN 0-517-88463-1

10   9   8   7   6   5   4   3   2

First Edition

CONTENTS

HOW THIS BOOK WILL HELP YOU
RAISE YOUR CHILD

Congratulations on making the time to read this book. Like most parents, you are probably so busy raising your child that you have little time to get the resources and reinforcement to maintain the stamina required for what has to be the most important job on earth. This quick parenting how-to manual will help if you have few precious moments to read, don't want to be preached to, and want encouragement for all you're doing on your child's behalf.

Change Your Child's Behavior by Changing Yours is based on two premises:

1. IF YOU WANT TO CHANGE YOUR CHILD'S BEHAVIOR, YOU HAVE TO CHANGE YOURS FIRST.

Kids imitate what they see and repeat behavior that is rewarded—whether it's with positive or negative attention. If you want your child to alter his actions, you have to change your adult reactions to him.

2. MOST INAPPROPRIATE BEHAVIOR IS DEVELOPMENTALLY APPROPRIATE. A CHILD ACTS LIKE A CHILD BECAUSE SHE IS ONE!

If you had a better understanding of what was occurring physically and mentally with your child, it might help you approach "behavior problems" differently and enjoy a more positive result. The more age-appropriate power and control you give your child, the more control you'll gain as a parent. Then, when you have to pull rank, you'll win with your child's self-esteem intact.

We use a lighthearted approach to teach these two very serious, life-altering lessons. And we've designed this book to be easy to use. You can breeze through the book front to back, or choose the chapter that most interests you at the moment.

The book offers tools for coping with thirteen of the most nagging problems involving children ranging in age from birth to about age six. Each chapter gives quick insights into why your child is behaving a certain way and provides ideas for handling the situation in a positive manner. As one parent put it, "I know what I'm supposed to do, but I don't know how to do it." This book gives you the words and the tools you may not be able to find on your own.

The chapters begin with a universal scenario of a child/parent tug-of-war called "Sound Familiar?" This is followed by "The Tune Your Child Sings," a description of what's occurring with the child developmentally, which serves as the impetus to that particular behavior.

Next, the chapters feature a "Low Notes" section, a quick look at typical reactions any red-blooded parent might have to the problem presented—but which too often lead to negative interactions. A fun insert called "Stop! Rewind Your Own Tape" relates the child's behavior to a very similar adult behavior in a somewhat parallel situation. This brief reflection is designed to motivate you to rewind the tapes of your own experiences and admit that your adult reactions are different from your child's reactions only because of your maturity, experience, inhibitions, or fear of embarrassment. (Come on, admit it. Adults throw tantrums, pout, take revenge, and refuse to cooperate. It's just that our actions are cloaked in adult rhetoric, gestures, and behaviors.)

The next section, "High Notes," offers fresh alternatives for reacting to your child's behavior. These techniques will empower you to give your youngster control and respect—two key ingredients for behavior change. The remainder of each chapter offers information and tools to motivate you to change *your* behavior to get the desired results from your child.

Each chapter ends with a section called "Bibliotherapy," which provides the names of books you can read to your child that demonstrate the premise of the chapter. Reading to children is a necessary part of their development. It enriches language skills, expands horizons, and creates a time for physical closeness between parent and child. But books can also be used to teach lessons about social graces and appropriate behavior. Using books to point out to children the concepts of lying, manners, coping with sibling rivalry, or almost any other issue that comes to mind is a comfortable way for parents to open the door of communication with their child. There really are books on almost any subject you can imagine. Ask the children's librarian or children's bookstore owner to help you find a book on a specific topic.

When using books as a tool to teach children some of life's lessons, keep in mind that you must read the book completely to make sure that you are comfortable with all of the messages and the pictures. There are many wonderful books, but some may present a perspective that does not represent your own feelings or values. Stopping in the middle of the book because you were taken by surprise does not make for an enjoyable reading session and can frustrate you and your child. But the right book can be just the tool you need to help your child understand an important value.

We hope *Change Your Child's Behavior by Changing Yours* will give you renewed hope that there is pleasure in parenting. By learning how to change *your* reactions to your child, rather than trying to change your child, you will feel less of the angst and drudgery of parenting and have more energy and freedom to improve your family relationships.

PART ONE

PROACTIVE PARENTING

PUTTING PARENTS IN CHARGE:
CHANGING *YOUR* BEHAVIOR WILL CHANGE YOUR CHILD'S

PARENT JOB DESCRIPTION

To nurture and support a child in a loving, healthy, safe environment. To set and enforce boundaries and rules. To accept your child as a unique individual with needs, wants, and feelings separate from yours and others who live in the household. To provide opportunities for your child to be successful, to hold age-appropriate expectations for development and performance, and to accept failure as a challenge for change. To praise and reinforce positive behavior and growth.

Prerequisite: *Since there are no perfect kids, perfect parents need not apply.*

If you had known the breadth and responsibility of your role as a parent, would you have applied for the position? Hopefully your answer is yes because you realize that no parent can play the role perfectly. In fact, the words *perfect* and *parent* don't belong in the same sentence. For that matter, neither do *perfect* and *child*. But it is your responsibility as a parent to do your job in the best possible way—under the circumstances that arise—each day you are blessed to share with your children.

CHANGE *YOUR* BEHAVIOR FIRST

Being a successful parent lies in your understanding that it is hard work, often without any seemingly positive rewards. Without question, parenting is the most challenging job on earth. And it's a responsibility we often feel inadequate to handle. You're not alone if at times you find yourself questioning your role and your desire to continue in it. And don't feel bad if wails similar to these have passed your lips:

"Why are you doing this to me?"

"What did I do to deserve this kind of behavior?"

"I wasn't cut out for kids!"

"All I do is yell."

"I don't know if I'll survive until you're eighteen! (Or if you will!)"

When we're frustrated, we all but beg kids to change their behavior. But any parent of a two-year-old knows that you can't *really* make your child do anything against his will. When you force your kid into compliance, you usually suffer the consequences of battling wills, negative attitudes, and repeated inappropriate behavior.

You can avoid much of this if you understand that as the adult in the home, you must be in charge—not only of making sure your child is growing up in a loving, supportive environment, but of your reactions to each and every situation parenting brings. Though it may be a hard concept to accept—and something you don't want to hear—the truth is: *If you want to change your child's behavior, you have to change yours first.*

This means you must think through the ramifications of your behavior with your child *before* you act and before your child has a chance to *react*. When you change your reactions to your child from destructive to constructive, he will actually *want* to improve his behavior. And though teaching yourself new tricks isn't easy, it's a lot less harrowing than trying to *demand* that a three-year-old stop crying or a six-year-old never tell a lie again.

How you behave toward your child and other adults in his life teaches him appropriate (and inappropriate) social behaviors. You can't expect him to be loving and caring toward others if you, as his parents, are angry and hostile toward each other and/or them.

In addition to watching how you interact with people in your life, children also absorb how you live day to day, from coping with stress and adversity to expressing the thrill of joy and happiness. Like living video cameras, children record what they observe. Without the ability to distinguish right from wrong, they imitate that behavior—what they see is what they assume to be appropriate behavior. Young children have no basis for comparison, so they don't have the ability to filter out those behaviors that may be okay for adults but not for children. That's what makes it so easy for children to cuss or put others down. If Mom and Dad do it, it must be okay!

For every reaction you have toward your child, there is an equal response from the child that mirrors your tone, attitude, and demeanor. Kids are human and predictable. If you yell, your child will typically either shout back or fall apart in tears—neither of which is your desired goal. If, instead, you explain what needs to be done and the positive or negative consequences (age- and incident-appropriate), then you give your child a clear picture of the choices and an opportunity to take control of the situation. Model the behavior you want your children to mirror, and soon they will begin to change in response to you!

CONSEQUENCES TEACH KIDS TO CHANGE THEIR WAYS

Have you ever wondered, If only I could get my kids to behave for me as well as *they* get me to behave for them? Your child knows, based on your past responses, exactly what she has to do to get you to give in. If you stop acquiescing and stand firm on the big issues, it will be your child who alters her behavior to accommodate your will.

When you set up a system of rules and consequences (consequences are both good and bad, determined by the behavior), you turn the responsibility over to your child to determine the outcome. You are no longer the bad guy because you're not imposing a punishment. Your child's behavior indicates a choice for a certain outcome, and you're merely the enforcer of the outcome. For example, if you tell your daughter she can go out and play once she has cleaned up her toys, not doing the task and therefore not going out to play becomes her choice, not your punishment. You're no longer playing the role of warden.

Don't forget that however much your child fights to be in control, she subconsciously wants you to be in charge. In fact, kids often misbehave to force their parents into taking responsibility. They want and need you to be reliable and dependable, and to be able to count on you and your reactions.

Each time you state the consequences for a good or bad behavior and don't follow through, you confuse your child and hamper her ability to judge your response. You also open the door for more inappropriate behaviors, because when your child doesn't know what to expect, each day or activity becomes a new challenge of trial and error. Being consistent defines and reinforces your expectations. And, when your children know what your expectations are, it's easier to live up to them.

GIVING KIDS POWER IN MODERATION BREEDS COOPERATION

It's a heavy load for parents to have to be in charge all the time. This is not to say that parents can abdicate their adult role, it just means that you don't have to maintain *all* the power. If you were locked into a straitjacket and knew you couldn't break free, it wouldn't mean you still wouldn't try. The same is true for children. They fight against your power if they feel they have none.

So what can you do?

Give children as much power over their own lives as they are capable of handling. Of course, the power you give them will change and increase with the developmental process. But time invested in early childhood— teaching children to take responsibility for themselves— will pay enormous dividends as they go out into the world, adept at making good decisions.

As the adult, you have total control over what power you turn over to your child. Give him power only over things that match his age and ability and are not important to you or the family. That your child wants to sleep with his shoes on or eat his oatmeal with a fork is of little consequence in the real world. So why fight it just because you wouldn't do it? Your child will figure out that sleeping with so much paraphernalia is uncomfortable and eating oatmeal with a fork doesn't bring as much food to his mouth. He doesn't need you to tell him; experience is the best teacher!

Remember the times your parents warned, "Don't do that, you'll get hurt," but you didn't listen? You did it anyway because you didn't believe your parents and you had to learn right from wrong on your own. Though parents see it as their role to protect their child—and they absolutely should in some instances—those who try to shield their child from every negative consequence produce a child who has no coping skills for life's sometimes painful experiences.

You can have power in your relationship with your child by relinquishing some of it. Allowing your little one the freedom to make decisions and choices and to be an active participant in family dynamics gives him a sense of independence and, therefore, increases cooperation. Being an active participant means taking responsibility for being an involved member of the family. Parents often complain that their child thinks he can just skate through life while they put in all the effort to make the family and household run smoothly. When parents ask children to do their part, many kids act indifferent as if to say, "Hey, I'm just a kid. Getting ready on time, coming home when expected, cleaning the house, and sending thank-you notes are your job." If that happens in your house, chances are you inadvertently perpetuated this misconception and now are disappointed (all right, downright angry) when your child behaves accordingly.

Many parents selectively choose what family activities and events they want their child to participate in or be excluded from by virtue of his age or the parents' need to be powerful. The reality is that if you include children in the household operation from their earliest years, they will feel responsible, accountable, and valued. Children encouraged to participate—whether it's choosing what to have for dinner or picking the evening's entertainment (what video shall we rent?)—will take a bigger interest in the family's problems and solutions. Of course parents, because of their age, experience, and role as providers of economic means and well-being for the family, have more power than children. But that doesn't mean the children should have *no* power.

When parents make all of the rules and decisions that determine how the family operates, kids have no incentive to participate and are denied the opportunity to learn the inner workings of the family. If they are to become successful, independent adults/spouses/parents, kids must have opportunities to try out new skills within the safety of the family. And they must be able to make mistakes when the price is as cheap as it will ever be—when they are young.

When children are exempt from participating in the family dynamics, they may develop a false impression that their parents were put on the planet to serve them. While there is some degree of pleasure in being totally cared for and waited on, it serves no purpose for an adult future. In fact, it is frightening to children to feel they have more power in the family than the adults. Children who are feeling out of step with their parents often escalate inappropriate behavior as a means of reengaging their parents. They don't have any other means of re-connecting.

The more you do for your child, the more she expects you to do. And that often invites resentment and anger, especially today when life is filled with time and financial crunches and limited family and community support for raising children. Whether you ask your child her opinion about something and then act upon it or encourage her to make some of the inconsequential family decisions, you are saying that you, the most important person in her life, thinks she is a competent, capable family member. That is a powerful message to send to your child. And each time you do it, the foundation is set for future opportunities to build your child's self-confidence. Children who are treated as competent feel good about themselves and perpetuate positive behavior. And even if they repeat a successful experience until you are ready to scream (how many times can she dust the same table?), remember, it is through repeated efforts that children improve their skills. Keeping your tongue in check as children grow and attempt to help in their own way becomes even more important when the tasks become more difficult (remember when you had to learn how to diagram a sentence or learn long division?). Be patient, set reasonable, age-appropriate standards, and praise.

PRAISE MORE THAN YOU CORRECT

Let's face it, kids are trying and tiring. But parents often reinforce the wrong behaviors by giving attention to their children when they misbehave and ignoring them when they behave as desired. Of course, the rationale behind this is Why should I thank them for doing the right thing; that's not how life works. But think about it. If the only time your boss commented on your work performance was when you screwed up, what incentive would you have for doing a good job if it wasn't going to be recognized? On the other hand, if your boss made it a point of telling you how pleased she was with your work every time it was exemplary, not only would you have better coping ability for the times when it was not up to par, but the praise would be incentive for you to continue delivering good work.

Children thrive on the praise of their parents. Not idle praise, but sincere gratitude: "I really appreciate the way you behaved (or the work you did)." It lets them know what you like and dislike and establishes ground rules for future performances. Too often, parents think that children somehow know what makes them happy, and that when their children misbehave it is meant as a personal affront. In truth, children reinvent themselves daily, if not hourly, based on developmental evolution and the reactions and reinforcements of the adults in their lives.

LIVE, LEARN, AND LOVE

Adults enter parenthood with about as much skill and ability as their children enter the world, and mistakes are bound to happen. The wonderful thing about childhood is that it has a short memory. Children will forgive their parents for almost anything when the payoff in the long run is love and care. Don't let the foibles of your parenting discourage you. Mistakes you make today can be corrected tomorrow. Each day presents a new chance to get better at what you do.

The good news is that children accept their parents as mistake-making humans. Presenting yourself in any other light (perfection) leaves you open to falling far off the pedestal—and you will . . . it's only human. And that can be devastating to young children. It also sets up unrealistic goals for children to achieve and maintain perfection. Correcting your way through parenthood is a bona fide way to traverse the minefields.

Ultimately, remember you're not alone. Parents have come before you and parents will come after you. All bring something wonderful and different to their respective families. When you are feeling overwhelmed, reach out to those who may have experience—your parents, siblings, friends, and co-workers. And, in return, give back to those less-experienced parents, who wonder at times if they have the skill and stamina to go on. The information you receive from others won't always work, but it at least helps to know that you're not the only one who's walked through trouble's door. As different and unique as all children and parents are, there is a familiarity about all that we do as part of living and growing as a family. The chore will be easier and the reward greater when you can celebrate your successes with others!

WHY YOUR KID ACTS LIKE A CHILD:

MOST INAPPROPRIATE BEHAVIORS ARE AGE-APPROPRIATE

If you're the parent of a toddler or preschooler you've lived this scene. You're heading out of the shopping mall, hot and tired, when your child spots the ice cream stand. "I want ice cream!" he shouts.

"Not now. We're going home and will eat dinner soon," you say.

"But, Mommy, I want one . . . ," and the whining begins to escalate.

Thinking it will cause less of a scene if you just buy the treat, you give in to the lure of contentment, for both your sakes. You imagine moments of silence while your child is happily licking the ice cream and you're driving home with the air conditioner blasting.

In that fleeting moment, you added one more insight to your son's growing information bank on Mom. Ah ha, his mental computer registers. Now I know how to get Mom to buy me ice cream at the mall.

Or maybe you're the kind of parent who doesn't give in. Instead, you exert your authority: "Stop whining! You're acting like a baby!" Your child's behavior escalates into a temper tantrum, and you pull him kicking and screaming into the car. Your blood pressure rises off the chart, and your child has learned to combat anger with anger.

It's natural for a little one to be pouty or defiant when his will butts up against yours. But a parent who gives in to disobedience—either by always meeting a child's demands or by fighting back—is a parent who will forever be frustrated that his child acts, well, like a child!

Maintaining control is as hard for parents as it is for kids. Too often, parents act more like children than their children. They rant and rave and lose control. As harried and frustrated as you get, remind yourself that you must maintain your role as a rational adult. When you approach your child, ask yourself, Do I want to make my child pay a price and learn anger and hostility, or do I want my child to learn right from wrong and change his behavior?

In the case of the ice cream tantrum, there is a better alternative that lets you hold on to control in a way that respects the child. In an understanding but firm voice say, "I know you want ice cream, but you can't have it now." Each time the child cries out for ice cream, repeat the phrase like a broken record, in a tone that is steady and not angry. Not receiving any payoff from you, your little one will wear himself out and give up. And that's a whole lot better than wearing you down! The lesson his brain stores is: Mom means what she says. Whining and tantrums won't make her change her mind.

THINK OF YOUR CHILD
AS AN ALIEN LIFE-FORM

To a child, every day is new and exciting, bringing with it more skills to try, more abilities to test, and more milestones to achieve. If you knew the countless thoughts and questions whizzing through a child's mind, you'd be amazed that any of us grow up to be competent adults. As a parent, it's easy to take the job of raising children so seriously that you forget the wonder of childhood, not to mention how to enjoy the parenting experience and discover what a neat kid you're raising.

To put your child's naïveté into perspective, imagine she is an alien from another planet. (Okay, at times that assignment may not be so hard to do, but give it some thought anyway.) If an ET-type creature from outer space showed up at your door and wanted to fit into your world, would you rant and rave or raise a hand to spank it every time it did something wrong? Kids arrive in our family equally void of information about how to live life. But just because children are human, we think they are prewired at birth to know instinctively how to do things the correct way.

How would you react if on the first day of a new job, your supervisor showed you to your new office, pointed out the telephone and files, and left? With heart pounding and sweat beading on your brow, you'd frantically try to figure out what you were supposed to do and how to please your boss. You'd hunt for your job description, test things out, ask questions, and invariably make some mistakes. But what if your boss reacted to your unfamiliarity with the territory by saying, "You got the job, you should know what to do! You're fired!"

As parents, we often unconsciously have equally unrealistic expectations of our children. We forget they come into the world as blank slates, not knowing what's expected of them. We have to constantly remind ourselves that our kids are on a guided tour and we are the tour directors. The way they discover whether it's thumbs up or thumbs down is for us to tell them what is right and what is wrong and to serve as positive role models.

Here's a typical picture: A two-year-old draws on the wall. The parent, outraged by the mess, screams, "Bad girl! What a mess you made." The child cries at Dad's anger and quickly learns two lessons: I'm not worthwhile, and screaming is okay.

Wouldn't this be better: Dad composes himself in the heat of anger. He takes a minute to understand that his child is not intentionally wrecking the house, but is instead doing what any toddler would when faced with a crayon and a big open space begging for color. He deduces that he's probably not the only parent who's ever had to paint over a young Picasso's art. He takes a deep breath and gently removes the crayon from the child's hand, points to the wall, and calmly but firmly says, "No, you don't write on the wall, but you can write on paper. Do it again, and I'll take the crayons away." The message the child receives is: I made a mistake, but I can learn and go on.

Dad got what he wanted in a way that supported the child, and the child got what he needed—loving discipline with a logical consequence. By reacting this way, Dad corrected his toddler from a position of change, not a position of anger. The child has learned a valuable lesson, and Dad moves on guilt-free.

OVERCOME CHILDHOOD AMNESIA

Why is it that when we become adults, we suffer from amnesia concerning our own struggles growing up? On top of that, we also gloss over our adult weaknesses and foibles. Frustration rises when our babies lather their hair and the floor in banana puree, our toddlers refuse to share their toys, our preschoolers stick out their tongues, and our kindergartners tell lies. In the midst of our angst, we forget the heartaches we caused our parents years ago, and the trouble we cause our mates today! We expect our kids to see the world from our adult perspective and to follow the standards we set for ourselves. When our kids don't meet our expectations, we immediately express our disappointment. But when we make similar errors, we try to defend ourselves. Yes, even as a grown-up we make bad choices and pay the consequences. Take that hot fudge sundae you ate when you could have selected the bowl of raspberries instead! And what about last Friday, when you forgot to take out the trash and the ants invaded? Oh, yeah, even adults forget!

It's essential to step back from our dream of a law-and-order household and realize that most inappropriate behaviors are developmentally appropriate. If you don't, you'll waste precious time and energy trying to stop your kid from acting like a child and beating yourself up wondering what you're doing to encourage such deviant behavior.

Life as a parent is so much easier if you accept the hard fact that kids grow up into responsible adults only one baby step at a time. You can't rush nature and you can't fast-forward to age twenty-one. Kids act like kids because that's what they are. Children don't have the mental capacity to understand how the world works because they have a lack of life experience and maturity. They don't comprehend cause and effect, and so they'll dive headfirst into something simply because they don't know any better. It's only after the child tries something and the parent says, "Ah ha, we need to learn something new today" that the child will begin to understand right from wrong and the consequences of her choices.

But once is usually not enough—life's lessons have to be repeated again and again. Long-term change comes only when the child has developed to the point where information can be integrated into her thought process. No one gets upset when a new baby doesn't roll over after she's been home for two weeks, but we can't stand it when our preschooler doesn't get the message that she's to eat her food over the plate, even though we've told her dozens of times. Just as for an adult trying to learn a new computer program, with kids practice makes perfect (or at least, progress).

DON'T TAKE YOUR CHILD'S BEHAVIOR PERSONALLY

Your child looks like you; he acts like you. You've taught him just about everything he knows. When he's singing in the Thanksgiving recital, you swell with pride at the marvel you've created. But when he's pulling the tail of your neighbor's cat or giving his buddy a haircut with his preschool scissors, you have an urge to deny you've ever seen the kid before.

It's natural to feel personally responsible for your

child's behavior, because you know others are judging *you* by the way your child acts. But be careful. Taking your child's behavior personally can cause you to discipline for all the wrong reasons. Have you ever yelled a little louder or been a little more forceful because you were embarrassed by your child, or because you didn't want others to think you condoned the ill-fated deed? While your responsibility for your child's behavior will escalate as he becomes older (you'll be expected to fix the neighbor's broken window and the dented car fender will show up on your insurance premium), try not to let a young child's ploys and antics affect your confidence in your parenting ability.

Many parents also invest too much energy in correcting things that really don't matter. They lecture, scold, and yell so much about every misstep that the child grows immune to direction. If everything is off limits, the child will become so frustrated at not meeting your expectations that he'll just stop trying to do what's right. Who cares if your daughter wants a peanut butter and tuna sandwich? (It may make you sick, but it's her stomach.) Does it matter if your son wears his cowboy boots with his Hawaiian print shorts? (You wouldn't be caught mopping the floor in such a getup. But don't worry, he'll quickly develop better fashion sense if others make fun of him.) Why not let him go out in the rain and stomp in the puddles? What's wrong with letting her make mud pies? (You may not want the mess, but isn't a muddy sidewalk better than a bored child, and why not let her help you hose it clean?)

Remember, the decisions about what a child should eat, wear, or play are not about you; they're about the child. It all boils down to compromises of power and control. And the more parents give in on the inconsequential stuff, the more kids will listen to the things that really matter.

Choose your battles. Recognize that while there are some things you need to stand firm on, there are other instances when you really don't need to, and those unnecessary power struggles can damage your relationship with your child. The key to these compromises is loving guidance.

SET UP
EXPECTATIONS AND CONSEQUENCES

Whenever possible, remind your child of the behavior you expect *before* an event takes place. Be specific. Don't depend on generalities like "I want you to have good behavior at the movies." Instead use concrete examples such as "I want you to sit quietly during the movie. Whisper if you want to tell me something. Don't talk in a loud voice, because others in the theater won't be able to hear the movie."

As the adult, be sure you are not expecting too much of your child. Ask yourself if what you are requesting is something your child is capable of doing. For example, don't expect a four-year-old to be able to sit for two hours during a movie. Choose a short cartoon or an animal movie that will capture your child's interest.

Once you've established the ground rules, be sure your child knows the positive and negative consequences associated with following through on the expectations. Remember, good news is much more appealing and motivating than negative news, so focus on the upside. When you set up negative consequences, make them age-appropriate and as closely related to the misbehavior as possible.

Try to phrase what the child needs to do first so that he understands his actions and behavior are determining his fate—not you. "If you can sit quietly and talk in a soft whisper during the movies, you'll get to watch the whole movie. If not, we will have to leave early. And we will have to rent videos to watch at home before we try going to the movie theater again." (Remember, you always want your child to know he will have another chance to succeed.)

When you state a consequence, be sure it's something *you* can live with as a parent. If you are going to be disappointed because you had to leave *Pinocchio* before Geppetto gets rescued from the whale's belly, maybe you ought to go to that movie with a grown-up friend instead of your child!

When you have to act on a consequence, be as matter-of-fact as possible, so the consequence appears to be the natural result of your child's choice and not a result of your anger. "It looks like you're having trouble sitting still during this movie. Please get your jacket and let's go." When your child pouts and carries on, try to maintain as much composure as possible. Take his hand and lead him out of the theater.

When your child is settled down, you can encourage him with "When you are just a little older, we'll try going to the movie theater again."

At all costs, don't tell your child he blew his chance to do things right and please you; that will only set him up for continued failure. Remember, each moment brings with it a new chance to experience success. It's essential to discipline, but it's equally important to build your child's sense of self. It's a confident feeling—a positive outlook on life—that will give your child the ability to take risks and not fear failure.

While sometimes all the child needs is a reminder of the consequences, other times it's the follow-through that has the greatest chance of changing your child's behavior. The main purpose of using consequences is to allow your child to have a sense of control. You want him to be aware that his choices in life are in direct correlation with what happens to him. Each situation can be a valuable learning experience—if handled correctly.

If you're a parent who likes to count to three as a way of warning your child you want immediate action, make sure your child knows what will happen when you reach three: "I'm going to count to three and by 'three' you need to decide if you are going to walk to the car on your own free will or if I will have to carry you there" or "I'm going to count to three, and if you haven't started cleaning your room, you won't have time for a bubble bath." Again, use consequences that are as related to the event as possible. Avoid consequences you can't live up to, such as "If you don't clean up your room, I'll throw away all your toys." In the heat of the moment that sounds good, but later when you see that it means throwing away your money and leaving yourself a bored child, chances are you won't go through with it.

WHAT TO DO WHEN YOUR KID
ACTS LIKE A CHILD

Imagine . . . You take a day off of work to volunteer in your child's classroom. You sacrificed to be with your daughter, yet she pouts and throws a fit when you don't give her your undivided attention. She clings to you instead of participating in circle time and throws her cookie on the floor because she wanted chocolate chip, not peanut butter.

Knowing the teacher and other parent volunteers are questioning your parenting skills, you scold your daughter and give her that "wait till we get home" glare. You silently vow that you'll never put yourself through this humiliation again.

But wait! Instead of making rash generalizations in the heat of passion, here are five easy steps to put into action when your kid is acting like a *child*.

Choices
Hope and expectations
Ignore the little things
Learning opportunity
Desired behavior

1. CHOICES

When you reach the point at which your child is not acting as you desire, explain to her why the behavior is inappropriate and give several options for change. That way, you give her the power to make decisions.

Example: *"You're not acting nicely. Do you want Mommy to stay and work in your class, or do you want Mommy to leave?"*

2. HOPES AND EXPECTATIONS

Once your child tells you what she hopes for, explain the expectations that will have to be fulfilled in order for her desires to be met. Let your child know the positive and negative consequences associated with certain behaviors. State them calmly, in a matter-of-fact tone. Get her to understand cause and effect.

Example: *"Mom will be happy to stay and work in your class if you follow your teacher's rules and wear a happy face. If you don't do as your teacher says, I will have to leave."*

3. IGNORE THE LITTLE THINGS

Don't let your exasperation with your child take over so that you criticize every move she makes. Ignore little indiscretions by trying to understand the situation from your child's perspective. To cool down and get perspective, you may need to walk away from the immediate situation and take a minute or two by yourself to reflect.

Example: *Your daughter isn't acting up anymore in class, but she's not acting perfectly either. Rather than picking on her every move, tell the teacher you need to get some fresh air to calm down. Outside, count to twenty and take five or six deep breaths. As you take a moment to think, imagine what's going on with her.*

If you step away from the passion of the moment, chances are you'll discover that what you took as a personal affront was really your child trying to cope with a new situation: Mom in the classroom. As much as you want your daughter to act as pleasant as you know she can be, she is working overtime to please her teacher and her mom, and doing neither.

Try to think of a time that you, as an adult, acted similarly. Have you ever been in a situation with someone you are trying to impress and, much to your chagrin, repeatedly found your foot in your mouth? That's exactly what happened to your daughter, and she doesn't have the years of experience you have to extract herself from the sticky situation.

You might also take a minute to analyze what's got you so angry. Are you trying too hard to make a good impression? Are you worried what others will think? Once you've gained perspective, resume your interaction with your child.

4. LEARNING OPPORTUNITY

Remember, every event in your child's life is a learning opportunity. If your child acts according to your expectations—more or less—she has taken heed of what you said and decided to make the appropriate choice. But if your child tests you and doesn't make the right decision about how to act, make sure you follow through with the appropriate consequences. Your child needs to understand one basic principle: She chooses her behavior and her behavior dictates what happens to her.

Example: *Once you come back inside, your daughter again vies for your attention. She whines when you help others, and won't do what you or the teacher says. You ask yourself what your child needs to learn: Whine and get what I want, or whine and Mom will do what she said and leave. As hard as it is to do, go over to your daughter and explain, "Sweetie, I told you that if you couldn't wear a happy face, I wouldn't be able to work in your room. I'm leaving now,* *but we'll try again next week." Though you feel like Monster Mom crushing your child's spirit and know you're letting the teacher down, stick to your words so that your child will learn from her misbehavior.*

5. DESIRED BEHAVIOR

Following through on consequences is difficult, but if you do it in a rational, nonhostile way, your child will eventually begin to change her behavior. As easy as it would be to give in, your child will learn nothing if you do. Consistency and follow-through yield high returns.

Kids know when parents mean what they say, and they know when they can get away with pushing the limits. If you give your child choices, set up expectations and follow through if those expectations are not met. In turn, you teach your child that the world has rules and that when she chooses to follow the rules, good things happen. And when she decides not to follow the rules, less favorable things happen. When children realize that the choice of what they experience in life is theirs, they are empowered to make the right decision—and for the right reason: not because Mom or Dad told them to, but because their lives will be more pleasant. After all, everyone wants kids who can think for themselves and make smart choices.

PART TWO

TIPS FOR OVERCOMING YOUR KIDS' CHALLENGING BEHAVIORS

BEDTIME

"THERE'S A MONSTER IN THE CLOSET!"

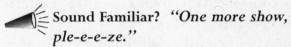 **Sound Familiar?** *"One more show, ple-e-e-ze."*

It's 8 P.M., and you announce that it's time for your five-year-old to go to bed. *"Let me watch one more show, ple-e-e-ze, Dad."*

"No, it's bedtime. Come on, you know you'll be too tired to get up in the morning if you stay up. Now go brush your teeth."

The Tune Your Child Sings: *"I'm not even tired."*

You've just asked your child to leave the warmth of his family and the fun of watching television to go to the last place in the world he wants to be when everyone else is up. He feels isolated and alone in his room, separated from those he loves. Besides, it's scary when the lights go out. And to top it off, he doesn't know he's tired.

Low Notes: *"He's dawdling again."*

Your child dawdles in the bathroom, and five minutes later you discover that he's made a toothpaste and water concoction in the bathroom cup instead of having brushed his teeth. "What did I tell you to do, mister?" you ask, angry that once again he's dragging out the bedtime ritual. "No time for a book now." Your

29

child whines, "No fair. I want a book." You return, "Don't talk to me like that. No book and that's final. Now, good night." You kiss him on the head while getting a sinking feeling that the last memory he'll have of you that day will be an unpleasant one.

Stop! Rewind Your Own Tape: *What adult wants to miss the fun?*

Have you ever had to leave a really fun party early when all of your friends got to stay? The entire drive home you wonder what you're missing. That's just how a child feels when he is separated from the rest of the family to go to bed and everyone else gets to stay up and continue what they're doing.

Or think of the times you've stayed up late to catch the end of a good movie, even when you knew you had to get up early for work. If we, as adults, do it, can we expect our children to turn in without a fuss when they don't think they're ready or when what's going on looks like more fun?

High Notes: *Outfox the conniver.*

Ease your child into the bedtime mode by preparing him for the nightly ritual. At 7:30 P.M., you might say, "You may watch one more TV show before it's time for a book and bed." When the time comes and he protests, acknowledge his feelings. "I know you like to stay up, but you need to get enough sleep so you won't be tired tomorrow."

If you know your child has a predictable pattern of postponing the inevitable, beat him to it. Instead of leaving him to his own devices in the bathroom, accompany him in there so he can't make his toothpaste concoction. If he gets scared when the lights go out, put a night-light in his room or keep a flashlight next to his bed and use it to look under the bed each night to assure him no monsters are hiding there. If calling out for a glass of water is his trick, place a glass of water on the nightstand before he makes his request.

TAKING THE STRESS OUT OF BEDTIME

Which bedtime routine do you think is best?

> You tell your child he must be in his room by 8 P.M., but he can crawl into bed whenever he is tired.
>
> You let your child know he must be in bed by 8 P.M., but he can read or listen to music until he is tired.
>
> You instruct your child he must be in bed at 8 P.M., be quiet, and have the lights out.
>
> You let your child fall asleep in your bed at 8 P.M.
>
> You lie down with your child at 8 P.M. and stay with him until he falls asleep.

The answer: Whichever behavior works best for you *and* your child.

Some children are morning people and need to be in bed early; others are night people and can't fall asleep before 10 P.M. no matter how hard they've played or how early they've awakened. There is no research that proves kids who sleep with their parents are any less secure than those who don't. And if you get pleasure from lying down with your child at night, don't let anyone tell you not to.

Here are ideas for ways to decrease the stress associated with bedtime:

INSTITUTE A BEDTIME ROUTINE AND FOLLOW THROUGH SO YOUR CHILD KNOWS YOU MEAN WHAT YOU SAY

Children thrive on routine. The more regular their schedule, the more easily they adapt. When children have inconsistent naps and irregular bedtimes, their bodies never regulate to a specific internal clock. But when events occur in a way children can count on—dinner, quiet play, brushing teeth, potty, storytime, snuggles, and lights out—their minds and bodies get into a pattern. They begin to get tired at the same time, and even when they don't, they become used to the schedule and accept it as the norm.

SET A REGULAR BEDTIME

With all the things that have to get squeezed into the limited evening hours, it's easy for bedtime to be haphazard. Chaotic schedules bode poorly for children heading off to bed at a reasonable hour. Though many parents often go sleep-deprived, young children cannot sustain too many consecutive nights of insufficient sleep. Setting and sticking to a set bedtime also gives parents the opportunity to have some quiet time for themselves before they fall into bed, exhausted from another day of too much to do and not enough hours to do it.

TRY TO EAT DINNER AS A FAMILY

Dinnertime is an opportunity for family members to catch up and share with one another (see the "Eating" chapter). Eating at approximately the same time each evening sets the tone for the rest of the night.

KEEP AFTER-DINNER ACTIVITIES LOW-KEY

Rather than encouraging high-energy activities after dinner, keep things low-key. The television need not be the only source of evening amusement. Suggest playing board games, reading books, or listening to music. Or make this a family time for teaching your child hobbies like sewing, knitting, woodworking, or drawing. In the summer take a walk, go for a bike ride, or sit outside and blow bubbles. When children know they're going to have your time and attention, they won't feel deprived and beg for more time when you say "nighty-night." And even though they will still want more attention, you won't have to feel as guilty!

OFFER YOUR KIDS A TRANSITION TIME

Give your child some transition time between what he is doing prior to bedtime and when he actually hits the sack. Make it an enjoyable experience that he looks forward to. And enjoyable usually means spending time with you doing such things as hearing a story, reading a book, singing soft songs, or saying prayers.

Though at the end of the day you're tired and want your child to just jump into bed, expecting that to happen unaided is unrealistic. You can choose to invest a few minutes to help her go to bed, or you can spend time in a power struggle that—even if you win—will leave you exhausted and angry. The latter also sets a pattern that will encourage nightly hassles.

BE PREPARED FOR DELAYS

Annoying as they may be, ploys to postpone bedtime mean your child wants to stay up and be a part of the family. (Who knows, something incredible might happen and she doesn't want to miss anything!) Putting your children to bed with drill-sergeant orders and zero tolerance for childhood wiles will only net tears and tantrums. You can make the nighttime ritual easier by anticipating and preparing for your child's delay tactics. If yours is the easily distracted type, who fools around while getting ready for bed, build that fudge factor into the time needed to get from wide-eyed to shut-eyed. If you can count on your little one to ask for a drink of water the minute she's tucked in, build that knowledge into your mental mind-set so you don't begrudge the request. (You might even want to bring the glass of water with you when you come in to say good night.)

Even though you may be prepared for delays, don't let your child stray off your schedule. Make sure she knows the bedtime rules and remind her of them— and the consequences of not following them—nightly if necessary. (A natural consequence might be: If you're late tonight, you will go to bed fifteen minutes earlier tomorrow.)

Expect your child to protest the rules, but don't give her the power to change them. Children don't have a sense of what's good for them. Wanting to stay up is normal, but it's not okay to deprive little bodies that need eight, ten, or twelve hours of sleep—rebuilding and refueling time. If you give in and your child wins, you all lose.

CREATE A POSITIVE ENVIRONMENT THAT CAUSES KIDS TO FALL ASLEEP BY CHOICE

When was the last time you went to sleep just because someone told you to? Children will fall asleep on their own if parents create a supportive environment to let them do so. There's nothing wrong if kids fall asleep to music or a story. Who says that it has to be quiet and dark for kids to drift off?

ASKING CHILDREN TO GO TO BED IS DIFFERENT FROM MAKING THEM GO TO SLEEP

Children have their own unique body clocks. You may be a morning person who greets each day with lightning speed, but who falls into bed asleep before your head hits the pillow. Your child, on the other hand, may be a night person, who has to pry her eyes open in the morning but could anchor the 11 P.M. news if you let her. Putting her to bed early or late does not affect her sleeping pattern.

Understand that you can't *make* kids go to sleep. Forcing them to behave in a way that satisfies your agenda but ignores their needs can open a floodgate of conflict. As a parent, you have a right to establish a pattern of behavior that is acceptable to you, but you must keep a clear vision of what your child is capable of doing. Let your child know that *you* decide what time she retires to her room, but *she* decides *when* she falls asleep. This reduces (but never completely eliminates) the war cry "I'm not tired!" Your response becomes "Fine, you don't have to go to sleep; you just have to be in your room. When you get there, you can read, sing, listen to music, or tell your dolls stories." This gives your child power over her life so she doesn't have to battle you for it.

STOP CHILDREN FROM COMING TO SLEEP IN YOUR BED—IF YOU DON'T WANT THEM TO

The jury is evenly divided on whether or not children should sleep in their parents' bed. One faction thinks children need to learn to be self-sufficient and independent; they have to learn to comfort themselves to sleep. If they rely on their parents for this comfort, they'll never learn to do it on their own. The other side says that children are young for only so long, and at some point in their early development they will want the privacy and separateness of their own rooms and beds.

There is no easy answer; parents must decide what is comfortable for them and stick to that decision. If having your family share the bed is joyful, go ahead. If, however, sleeping alone is important to you—for your health and sanity—and you want your children to sleep in their own beds, then enforce that rule.

Keep in mind that sometimes children need the comfort of their parents' closeness to ease them through a crisis (real or imagined). Forcing them away may send the message that you don't care. You might let your child fall asleep in your bed, and put her in her own bed once she's asleep. Or you might lie down with your child in her room until she falls asleep. Another possibility is to put a mattress on the floor in your room so your child is close but not too close. Then, slowly, wean your child from your room back into her own. The process may take a while, but you will reinforce your love and support for your child.

DON'T DISREGARD NIGHTTIME FEARS

If your child comes to you with nighttime fears, don't disregard them. They may not be real to you, but that doesn't mean they aren't real to your child. Give your little one some props that will help him feel powerful over things that may appear scary. If your child hits the "monsters in my bedroom stage," a nightly search under the bed and in the closet or a night-light or flashlight placed by the bed may be inexpensive ways to minimize the night-night tug-of-war. You might also mix up a potion of "monster-be-gone" or "monster away" (water and food coloring, or water and mouthwash) and give it to your child in a spray bottle so he can spray away his fears.

DON'T GIVE IN TO PLOYS TO KEEP YOU IN YOUR CHILD'S BEDROOM

Your child does not try to reel you back into her room to be annoying. In fact, she really doesn't understand how annoying it can be. She sees things only from her perspective, which is I love you and you love me, so shouldn't we be together? How can you want to send me off to bed and leave me all alone?

When you don't feel well or have had a bad day, isn't it nice to have someone you love envelop you like a down comforter until you drift to sleep? That's how your child feels.

If your child continually attempts to bring you back into his room, take a deep breath and just say no. If you've completed your regular rituals, set up a consequence for continued pleas for contact. It might be the loss of privileges the next night (story, song) or an earlier bedtime. Remember, your child likes being close to you and does not have the sophistication to understand that another day will bring more contact.

UNDERSTAND THAT IT'S NOT SELFISH TO WANT A FEW HOURS OF CHILD-FREE TIME TO UNWIND BEFORE YOU GO TO BED

Getting your child to bed early enough so you have time to yourself is good for the entire family. With the assurance that you'll have a few hours at the end of the night, you are more willing to make your child the priority in the early evening. Besides a time to recharge, time alone or with your spouse allows you to review the day's events and forgive and forget any of your child's indiscretions so that you may wake up renewed, ready to face a new day of togetherness.

POINTERS FOR MORNING REVEILLE

The opposite of the night-night woes is morning mayhem. Most kids don't like getting up and most parents hate having to put on their drill sergeant faces and barking commands to launch their kids into the world of the living. Keep in mind that if you take responsibility for waking up your child every day, your child doesn't have to be responsible for getting himself going. It becomes one more thing for you to oversee and one less thing of which he has ownership.

Wake-up time is critical when parents and children have to be out of the house to get to child care, school, and work. Without those have-tos, children would wake up when their bodies were ready. As with bedtime, a regular routine and morning rituals are important to maintaining a get-out-of-the-house schedule that meets everybody's needs and obligations. Here are a few pointers to make the morning routine a more palatable way to start the day.

USE AN ALARM CLOCK TO MAKE YOUR CHILD RESPONSIBLE FOR GETTING UP

Children under age four usually need their parents' hand in getting ready in the morning. But once your child turns four, set an alarm clock for him. Leave plenty of time for your little one to reach consciousness, get up, washed, dressed, and into the kitchen for breakfast (if that is part of your daily routine).

If possible, have a few minutes for togetherness before everyone goes their separate ways. It's very disconcerting to be whisked from the bed and out into the cold morning without some family time. For young kids, the day can seem very long when they are away from the ones they love.

SET MORNING ROUTINES THAT YOUR CHILD ENJOYS

Set boundaries and priorities in the morning with built-in rewards for achieved goals. It's smart to set a rule that your child get washed, dressed, and comb his hair before diving into his favorite cereal or playing with toys. If you see your child getting off course, remind him of what he *can* do once he has done what is required.

FOLLOW THROUGH WITH APPROPRIATE CONSEQUENCES IF YOUR CHILD IS NOT READY ON TIME

When your offspring consistently dawdles, it's time to get tough and set strict consequences. You should not become the victim—late for work—because of your child's inability to get into gear. If you let your child rely on you to dress him when he is perfectly capable of dressing himself, you take on one more responsibility and he takes on one less. And if your child fools around and you rush in angrily at the last minute to dress him, he'll expect you always to come to his rescue.

You can help your youngster by instituting a routine to accomplish morning rituals faster. This might mean requiring that the next day's clothes be set out the night before or that baths be taken at night. But when your child isn't ready on time, you must follow through with meaningful, natural consequences. If your daughter (who loves breakfast) misses her cereal a few days in a row, not for punishment but because she "chose" not to get ready when asked, she may feel the consequences of her actions and speed up her morning act. And if you take your son, who refused to get dressed, to school in his pj's, chances are the snickers of other kids will be the key to an attitude adjustment.

This is not done in anger. The goal is simply to help them learn that they have responsibilities they must live up to—for their sakes and the sake of the entire family—or experience the consequences.

When your child is successful, make sure you express your joy and point out the benefits of having accomplished the morning tasks—second helpings of cereal or newfound time to watch cartoons.

RESERVE A FEW MOMENTS FOR YOURSELF EVERY MORNING

If getting everybody out of the house in a timely manner leaves you exhausted before the day begins, you might need to adjust *your* schedule. Going to bed earlier and getting up earlier may give you the time you need to start your day in a saner manner. And if morning mayhem continues, have a family meeting and assign responsibilities so that you share the family's day-starting obligations.

BIBLIOTHERAPY

There's an Alligator under My Bed, by Mercer Mayer
There's a Nightmare in My Closet, by Mercer Mayer
Time for Bed, by Mem Fox
To Sleep, by James Sage
A Child's Good Night Book, by Margaret Wise Brown

DRESSING

"POLKA DOTS AND STRIPES *DO* MATCH!"

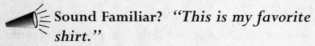 **Sound Familiar?** *"This is my favorite shirt."*

Your preschooler wants to pick her own clothes for school. She puts on a yellow flowered shirt, red striped shorts, green polka-dot socks, blue tennis shoes, and a purple plaid headband. "Sweetie, do you think those match?" you ask, trying not to laugh.

"I think they look pretty," she says confidently.

"Honey, you can't wear stripes, flowers, and polka dots together."

"But I want to," your four-year-old angel says, and begins to cry.

The Tune Your Child Sings: *"I want to make my own decisions."*

To a young child, there's little difference between playing dress-up and getting dressed for school. She grabs whatever attracts her attention with no notion of what matches. All she cares about is that she likes each item individually and if that's the case, why shouldn't they look good together? To a little one just acquiring the maturity to choose what *she* wears and to wear it means a lot. It's a step of independence that feels pretty good.

Low Notes: *"I can't let my child look like that."*

You can't stand to see your beauty queen go to school looking so funny. Besides, the flowered shirt has a small hole in the shoulder—the perfect excuse to get her to change! "You can't wear that blouse, Stephie," you say kindly. "Mom's got to fix the hole. Besides, why don't you pick the red shirt that matches those shorts? It will look so pretty!"

"I want this one. I don't care about the hole," Stephie states. "This is my favorite blouse."

"I won't let you go to school looking like that. Now put on this red shirt. Come on, it's time to go." You take off Stephie's favorite flowered blouse, but not without hurting her feelings and pulling her hair in the buttons as you try to work with an uncooperative child. She reluctantly lets you put on the red blouse, but now instead of wearing a proud smile she sulks all the way to school. You watch her walk sullenly into class and wonder if she would have been better off if you weren't so worried that her lack of taste reflected poorly on you.

Stop! Rewind Your Own Tape: *Remember the dress he gave you that you never wore?*

Has your spouse ever given you a new outfit he painstakingly picked only to have you secretly hate it? You'd never speak the truth, but frankly it looked like something out of a 1954 Sears catalog. While you tried to show appreciation, you knew you wouldn't be caught cleaning the kitchen in that getup. Chances are, you either pretended it didn't fit and returned it, or relegated it to the back of the closet, eventually putting it in the discard pile.

Most of us believe that how we dress reflects who we are, and we don't want other people imposing their tastes on us. Discriminating taste in an adult is chic, but in a child it's disobedient. Is there a shade of inequality there somewhere?

♪ High Notes: *"Who cares if my four-year-old isn't a fashion plate?"*

You swallow hard when you see your child's wardrobe creation. You rationalize that it's a mother's duty to teach her what matches and what doesn't, but not at the expense of a budding ego and independence. "Honey, most people don't wear stripes, flowers, and polka dots at the same time," you say, hoping to impart some fashion sense. "But I like them. This is my favorite shirt," she says. "Would you like to wear the red shirt, instead?" you question, hoping she'll see the error in her taste. "No, not today," she says emphatically.

Though you wish you had won this clothes battle, it's not worth a fashion war. You give in reluctantly. "Okay. Let's go to school." And you bite your tongue during the entire car ride. Even though you secretly wish you could be invisible, you take your child into preschool and say nothing until Stephie is out of earshot on the playground. Then you comment to the teacher, "What an outfit she put together today! She thinks she looks great, and that's all that really matters."

One of the biggest battle lines drawn between parents and children starts at a very early age when kids begin establishing their own sense of self and want to choose what they wear. For parents, this often leads to horrified protests when children show up at the breakfast table in their latest creations. You may not be sure whether to laugh, cry, scream, or demand that your child change into something more suitable!

Telling kids what to wear is a tough call. For some occasions proper attire is, well, proper, and you can't let your children detract from the affair. On the other hand, sometimes it just really doesn't matter, and kids will learn for themselves when their peers let them know the outfit just doesn't work.

Here are some suggestions for how to choose your battles and avoid going to war over the clothes issue:

AVOID WRAPPING UP YOUR SELF-ESTEEM IN YOUR CHILD'S APPEARANCE

Admit it. The real issue isn't what your child wears but what *other* people think about what your child wears and how it reflects on you. Right? Once you face the fact that no one else really cares that your son wears the same pair of blue jeans three times a week or your daughter insists on wearing hiking boots with dresses, you can relax and enjoy the pure joy young kids are afforded by not being tied to social mores.

REALIZE THAT MOST KIDS HAVE NO FASHION SENSE

Children generally choose their clothes based on comfort and individual appeal. They do not put "outfits" together. That's what parents do. In fact, for children, every day is make-believe. Clothing is just an accessory or prop and has no real significance. As many a parent will tell you, children are born nudists and given half a chance, would sooner run naked through the yard than worry about the conventional wisdom that surrounds clothing.

UNDERSTAND THAT CLOTHES ARE ONE WAY YOUR CHILD CREATES HIS OWN PERSONAL STYLE AND IDENTITY

There are so many things you and your child will fight about; don't let clothes be one of them. It will only boil down to a power struggle, and it's one you can't win. Even if you get your child to dress according to your standard of what's appropriate, he'll look for other ways to rebel to prove you can't control his life. Clothing is a wonderful way for people to express themselves, from the outgoing and flamboyant to the passive and calm. How children dress speaks volumes about how they perceive themselves. It is an avenue for creativity and experimentation, and should be encouraged.

ENCOURAGE BEHAVIORS YOU CAN SUPPORT

While you can't make your child bend to your wishes, you can encourage behaviors you support. When your child is young and you buy the clothes, you have control over the wardrobe. You can help your child select her clothing and can code separate articles with identifying marks that when matched create a complementary outfit. Or when you help your child get dressed, ask questions like "What colors go with blue?" or "What shirt in your closet matches these shorts?"

Remember, you are your child's fashion model and

consultant. If you utilize the "hunt through the laundry basket" mode of getting dressed, your little one will imitate you. So don't get upset if she looks a little disheveled. If, on the other hand, you make it a point of hanging up clothes after wearing them (and you're to be envied if you do!) and putting your shoes in the closet in an orderly fashion, your youngster will be more organized about the way she approaches getting dressed.

EXPECT YOUR CHILD TO REBEL WHEN ASKED TO CONFORM TO YOUR STANDARDS

Children go through stages when they do the exact opposite of what their parents want as a way of establishing their personal likes and dislikes. If you overreact, you will encourage your child's defiance. If, instead, you keep a cool head and an amazing sense of humor, you can help your child find herself without ridicule. "My, my," you might say, "that is surely an interesting outfit you have put together today!" When your child sees that her behavior does not escalate yours, she'll realize it's not worth doing something contrary to your wishes, because nothing happens when she does.

TAKE KIDS WITH DISCRIMINATING TASTES SHOPPING WITH YOU

Shopping without kids is always easiest. But as children reach and grow beyond preschool years, they develop distinct opinions about what they wear—often dictated by current fads and peer behavior. When kids begin worrying about how they look, it may be best to take them shopping with you. Better to make compromises together in the store than to do battle each morning in front of the closet.

Plan a time when you're well rested and have ample stamina for the task. If you are tired and short-tempered, you're begging for misery. Be specific with your child about what you're looking for, and stay on target. While he may try to sway you to items not on your list, keep focused.

As you look through racks of children's clothing, talk to your youngster about fabrics that are long-lasting and about how to build multiple outfits from several individual pieces. The more you talk about styles of clothing, colors, and patterns that work together, the more your child will begin to develop a fashion sense.

DON'T WORRY WHEN KIDS IMITATE THE OPPOSITE SEX

Developing a sense of self for young children requires strong role models for them to imitate. But don't go wild if your son puts on Mommy's shoes and dress or your daughter wants to wear Daddy's tie and hat. Kids enjoy mirroring the people they know and love. They have an understanding that boys and girls are different, but that is the extent of their gender knowledge. There is no hidden agenda in their play. Children are equally likely to play Beauty as they are the Beast, Snow White as they are Prince Charming. Drawing attention to or making fun of your child for cross-gender dress-up raises more questions than it answers and leaves your child confused and, perhaps, frightened. If children are encouraged only to play in their own gender role, it limits them to following a life path based not on potential and ability but on some arbitrary standard of what men and women can and should do.

INTRODUCE KIDS TO THEIR HAMPERS

Children, by nature, allow others to take care of them. They think it's their right and their due, so don't be amazed when dirty clothes don't make it to the hamper. You can, however, set rules about how their clothes should be treated. Teach kids early on that dirty clothes don't get piled on the floor. You might employ a reward system: "I'll be happy to read you a book, just as soon as your clothes are in the hamper."

Once kids get the hang of it, it's easy for them to use the hamper as a dumping ground. Young children usually wear an item of clothing only once—even if it's just for an hour—before tossing it in the dirty laundry. It's just easier to wad clothes up and throw them into a basket than to take the time and effort to hang them up. Give kids some guidance to develop a laundry mentality that meets your needs and standards. You may want your child to wear his clothes only once, or it might be suitable for him to wear some clothes more than once if they aren't soiled. As your child learns to reason, teach him how to examine his clothes to determine if the laundry bell has them down for the count.

You can't rely on young children to take full responsibility for laundry day, but they can help. When you're going to do the wash, ask your child to be responsible for carrying his dirty clothes to the washer. When the laundry is done, exaggerate your pleasure in having clean clothes to wear. When your child puts on newly laundered clothes, tell him how nice they look and smell.

These actions support and reinforce your expectations. Most children will repeat behaviors that elicit positive attention from their parents.

SET EXPECTATIONS FOR IMPORTANT EVENTS

When a situation arises in which you want your child to dress a special way, explain the reasons why certain attire is appropriate and why the outfit she wants to wear is not. Acknowledge your daughter's wishes to dress differently, and then reinforce your expectations. Whether it's a Sunday-morning dress or holiday dinner apparel you desire, setting guidelines is okay as long as there are other times when your child has the freedom to dress as she chooses.

Have you ever looked at old photos of yourself dressed in ensembles that at the time you thought were too cool for words, only to wonder how your folks ever let you out of the house? Beauty is in the eye of the beholder and children and parents don't always have the same ideas about what looks good. Your relationship with your child is too precious to let something as insignificant as styles and patterns come between you.

BIBLIOTHERAPY

Benjamin Bigfoot, by Mary Serfozo
Mathew and His Dad, by Arlene Alda
Red Is Best, by Kathy Stinson
The Purple Coat, by Amy Hest
The Wonderful Shrinking Shirt, by Leone Castell Anderson

EATING

"I'M ALL DONE."

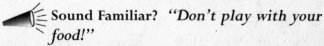 **Sound Familiar?** *"Don't play with your food!"*

Your two-and-a-half-year-old has just tossed a handful of peas to the floor. "Katie, stop playing with your food," you say, exasperated by the mess. But just as you do, she splatters mashed potatoes everywhere. Angered that your carpet and table are a mess, you spring for the sponge and towel.

The Tune Your Child Sings: *"Wow! Peas are just like little green balls!"*

Katie's tummy feels full and she's no longer interested in eating. Ah, but look at those bright colors and interesting shapes on the plate, she thinks to herself. Wow! This white fluffy stuff is just like play-dough, and those little green things are cute little balls! What fun!

Low Notes: *"What a mess you've made!"*
Back with cleaning tools in hand, you brusquely pick up your daughter. The anger in your face and your quick moves send her to tears. "What a mess you've made," you scold. "Go to your room for a time-out. There will be no cake for you tonight!" Deprived of the family's company and dessert, she cries even louder.

Your peaceful meal has been ruined, and by the time you clean up the mess you have no appetite left.

▰ Stop! Rewind Your Own Tape: *Haven't you asked for a doggie bag?*

It's happened to you. You've gone out for dinner, but by the time you finish the appetizer, soup, and salad, you have no room for the entrée. So you ask the waiter for a doggie bag. But hold it. How would you feel if the waiter said, "Oh no, I'm sorry, you can't get up from the table until you've eaten everything on your plate." You'd protest loudly as you launched into a litany of your legal rights. Parents stop eating when they don't want any more, but we often don't give our children the right to do the same.

♫ High Notes: *"When you're done eating, use your words."*

When the first handful of peas falls to the floor, you turn to your child and say firmly, "When you are done eating, use your words to say, 'All done.' " Then, taking her plate away quickly, you reinforce, "I can see you are finished. You may stay at the table and be with the family, or you may go get one toy and play quietly by the table."

Now, instead of throwing down the gauntlet in anger and causing your child to fight back as a matter of survival, you've stopped the negative action and given her two choices. And instead of angrily taking away the dessert, you can instead set up a rule. "If you decide to leave the table before everyone is done eating, your mealtime is over and you'll have to wait until tomorrow to have dessert. Do you understand?'' If the child protests, don't escalate her anger by yelling. Calmly say, ''Remember the rule.'' And the next time, simply reinforce your position with the simple question, ''What is the rule?'' After a while, even the most stubborn child will give in when Mom and Dad don't feed the frenzy with angry words and actions.

What parent hasn't forced a child to eat when he wasn't hungry, punished a child for bad table manners, and fought the ''good'' food/''bad'' food war? When will moms and dads learn that try as they may, they can't make children eat!

Mealtime can be an enjoyable experience or *Apocalypse Now!* It should be a time for good nutrition and family bonding. The healthy attitude toward food that you help your child develop is a mind-set that will stay with him for a lifetime and help him avoid future eating problems and food phobias. There are so many feelings linked to food that it's easy for the eating battle to escalate beyond the dining-room table to the deepest, darkest expressions of love and hate. Parents who put a premium on making sure their child wins the clean-plate award can create a child who refuses to eat as a matter of control. It is often the parents who worry about their child's eating habits who bribe their child with junk food and rationalize that ''at least the child is eating something''! In essence, the child is holding the parents' love hostage and the parents are making bad choices.

Here are a few suggestions for making peace with food in your family.

GIVE KIDS A SENSE OF CONTROL AND CHOICE OVER FOOD

As the parent in charge of your child, your job is to provide opportunities for him to make good decisions, and mealtime is an excellent occasion for that. Give your child (or let him serve himself) a little bit of everything and let him choose the order in which he will eat them. You can certainly establish any rules you want regarding second helpings. For example: "You can have seconds of anything after you have eaten everything on your plate" or "After one glass of milk you drink water, so savor your milk rather than gulp it down." (Milk is a real stomach filler, but it doesn't offer enough nutrients that are available from other foods.)

DON'T FORCE KIDS TO EAT WHEN THEY'RE NOT HUNGRY

In infancy, food is a matter of survival. But even then, some babies are intermittent eaters, taking forever to finish one bottle, while others snuggle up to the nipple and complete the meal in a joyful gastronomical experience. Parents of poor eaters often take their children's behavior personally. And those feelings of frustration and disappointment can continue and impact the parent and child for a long time.

Parents must understand that each individual has his own stomach capacity and timetable. You cannot set your child's "eating clock" based on your personal timetable or some arbitrary standard—It's 6 P.M., so it's time to eat. Similarly, kids may not eat as much as we think they should. They have small stomachs and need only a little bit of food at each meal throughout the day. Children who are appropriately active have an internal food meter that tells them when they're hungry and when they're full. That amazing machine, the body, will take in what it needs and then send a message to the brain that says, Okay, you're done. If you load your child's plate down with more food than she can eat and then require her to sit and eat it all, you are laying down a challenge that you can't win. Conversely, if you try to control your child's food intake with some mis- guided notion of how much is appropriate and don't give her enough, she will always be hungry, which isn't good, either. Let your child be your guide as to por- tion size. Just make sure the helpings—however small —represent the food groups you want your youngsters to eat from.

DON'T MAKE AN ISSUE ABOUT KIDS WHO DON'T WANT TO EAT

Food can become a major source of anger in a household when a child doesn't feel like eating and parents beg and bribe. That puts the child in total control of mealtime. The entire focus of attention during dinner is how much, if any, Junior has eaten. Mom and Dad, and any siblings, now dance to the tune played by the child, who has learned that not eating gets him undivided attention. And it can reach the point where nobody looks forward to sitting down to dinner.

When your child chooses—for whatever reason— not to eat, don't make a big deal of it. You can require him to stay at the table with the family, eating or not, or you can allow him to leave the table, but you cannot make an issue out of it. This way, your child learns he is solely responsible for his food intake.

REALIZE YOUR CHILD WON'T DIE IF SHE MISSES ONE MEAL

When your child doesn't comply with family mealtime rules, it may be best to deem *her* mealtime over. She may have to sit at the table while others finish, or may be excused from the table to clean up her toys or to take a bath. Don't worry about starvation. If the meals you serve to your little one contain the necessary nutrients her body needs over time, missing a meal will not have a major impact.

DON'T EQUATE FOOD WITH LOVE

Statements like "If you loved me, you'd eat your dinner" or "I worked hard to prepare this meal and that's how you show me your appreciation?" teach children that eating food is an expression of love. Think of all the people who eat compulsively and blame their eating behavior on having to clean their plates. Remember, the only role food should play is to nourish the body. It's the time with one another that warms the heart.

BE CREATIVE IN GETTING GOOD FOODS INTO YOUR CHILD

Don't be so dogmatic about what your child should eat that you neglect to find creative ways to get her the vitamins and minerals she needs. If there is a food your child refuses to eat (like vegetables), find substitutes with the same nutrients. Your daughter may not eat a tomato but will drink tomato juice, or may not eat carrots whole but will eat them shredded when they are mixed with raisins. You can also set rules that encourage your child to eat well by serving the healthier foods first. For example, serve a small dinner salad before the pasta and encourage your child to eat it by saying, "When you have finished your salad, I'll bring you your spaghetti." Once you make the rule, don't give in. If your child plays with the lettuce and doesn't eat it, take away the salad and excuse the child from the table with the words "Oh, it looks like you don't want any spaghetti tonight." Chances are, knowing she won't get the pasta, she'll change her mind and dig into the salad!

DON'T MAKE A BIG DEAL WHEN INTRODUCING NEW FOODS

Serve your child something new to eat without a lot of fanfare. Make sure there are other familiar and friendly foods available at the same time, otherwise the new food takes on an entirely different value of control and you can't win.

Remember that young children react more to appearance and texture than they do to taste. On the other hand, little ones do not have sophisticated taste buds, and foods that you love may not be tasty to them. Don't take food rejection personally, and don't write off a food because it wasn't tried or enjoyed the first time you served it. Keep reintroducing it.

ESTABLISH RULES FOR STAYING AT OR LEAVING THE TABLE

If you require your child to stay at the table when he is done eating, you may make your life miserable once he hits the boredom stage. On the other hand, if you allow him to leave the table, you run the risk of having him race through his meal or not eat because he'd rather watch TV or play.

Establish rules for dinner table attendance and endurance. You might allow a young child to have a small toy or book at his high chair to keep him amused and safe while you eat your dinner. An older child can participate in family discussions and learn good manners while he sits at the table. If you allow your child to leave the table, you might say that the only activities available during mealtime are reading a book or playing with a puzzle; no TV, video games, etc.

SET AND ENFORCE FOOD RULES ONCE CHILDREN LEAVE THE TABLE

What do you do when your child says he's full and asks to leave the table—even though he's barely touched his food—and then comes back a short time later pleading starvation with near-death antics? First, remind him of when the kitchen is open and when it is closed *before* he leaves the table. For example, at dinner you might say, "When you leave the table, your mealtime is over. No more food will be served to you until breakfast." Then, regardless of his Academy Award–winning performance of child on his last legs, stick to your rule.

If your child comes back five minutes after you've put away the last dish and begs for another chance at dinner, acknowledge his pain: "I can imagine you might be hungry considering how little you ate at dinner. I'll make sure to save the largest banana for you for your before-bedtime snack." This will not sit well with your child, who will pull out all stops to get you to provide food, including threatening to call the child-abuse hotline. Hand him the phone and say, "Feel free."

If you give in to histrionics, your child learns what to do to get to eat whenever and whatever he wants. That means you give up another piece of your control and sanity. When they see that even the most talented performance will not get them what they want, they will think twice before leaving the table without filling their tummies.

Throwing out a few good "I told you so's" ("I told you you'd be hungry if you left the table") will not improve anything either. This histrionic behavior is debilitating and exhausting to parents. More often than not it leads parents to throw their hands up in disgust and give in. You've given your child just what he wanted: He gets to eat at whim and gets you to run an all-night café. With that kind of success, he can't help but think, "Now, that's a behavior worth repeating."

WATCH WHEN YOUR CHILD EATS TO IDENTIFY APPETITE-SPOILING BEHAVIORS

It's possible that your child really wasn't hungry at dinnertime because she's operating on a time clock different from yours. Step back to see if you can detect an eating pattern that's contrary to what works for most members of your busy family. Is your child having an afternoon snack too late in the day? Are you and your youngster coming home positively starving and grabbing snack food to tide you over? No wonder when you sit down to dinner your child has no interest in eating!

Instead, make your before-dinner snack part of your

dinner. Have a plate of sliced vegetables and dip or fruit and cheese ready for eating while dinner is being prepared. Whatever food you choose, make sure it fits into a well-balanced, nutritious meal. Then dinner can be much simpler and serves as a time of togetherness rather than a time of food hassles.

MAKE PREPARING DINNER A FAMILY EVENT

Your dinnertime routine itself may be the culprit of mealtime mayhem. Is your child starved more for your attention than for food? Do you send her off to occupy herself while you become a martyr in the kitchen, alone and angry that you're still working? Don't let that happen. Restructure mealtime events to include your child —even a three-year-old can help in the kitchen. Give your youngster your attention as part of the family routine so she doesn't have to battle with you to win it. Whether it's washing vegetables, folding napkins, setting the table, or more, children are perfectly capable of assisting their parents in the running of the house. To exclude them sets up a perfect environment for numerous tugs-of-war that leave both sides bloodied and battered.

DON'T LET JUNK FOOD BE A DIETARY STAPLE

One of the biggest crises facing parents is the influence of television advertising. From fast-food burgers and hot dogs to potato chips, sugarcoated cereal, and candy, children are bombarded with messages for foods that may satisfy their taste buds but don't help their growing bodies get the proper nutrition.

One of the first things you can do to minimize how

much junk food your child eats is to be a good role model. If you give your child vegetables while you're eating something else, she understands that vegetables are not desirable. If your child sees you reaching for the chips, cookies, cake, or candy, she will become confused and crave those foods.

Second, rather than excluding all the fun, unhealthy foods from your child's life, incorporate them as part of a total dietary plan. If you ban treats from your home and your child, not only do those foods take on an almost golden hue, but your child will overdose when exposed to them.

You can't shelter your kid forever. She will be exposed to candy, cake, ice cream, and other less-nutritious foods the first time she goes to a birthday party or has a snack at a friend's house. Foods become powerful only if you bestow power upon them. Your child won't think much about sugary and salty snacks if they are treated the same as other foods. And don't use the fun foods as a bribe to get your child to eat healthy foods. If you do, you only teach your child that the healthy foods have something wrong with them and need to be washed down with the good stuff!

DON'T USE FOOD TO CONSOLE OR CELEBRATE

Food should not be used to chase away pain or celebrate joy. That's not to say you shouldn't ever eat when you're sad or happy. Just don't use it as a pacifier or reward: "Wow, you drew a beautiful picture, let's go have some ice cream" or "Gee, your Snuggy Bear lost an ear, let's go have some ice cream." Feeling pain and experiencing joy are natural. Often, the real reason we use food is that it fills the empty spaces in our lives. What your child needs is your love and closeness.

TEACH MEALTIME MANNERS

A child needs to learn mealtime manners, but you don't achieve that goal by withholding meals as a punishment. What does sending a child to bed without supper have to do with hitting baby brother at the dinner table? Keep in mind the goals of mealtime. It should be a time for the family to share their lives and for individuals to rejuvenate the body. Try to save the punishing for later.

However, as a last resort, if your child can't behave at the dinner table, you can deprive him of your attention. Make him eat alone in the kitchen, or wait until everyone else is done. But don't deprive him of food.

Institute separate and special times for teaching your child how to use utensils and a napkin, when to say please and thank you, and to ask to be excused. Your child will learn these behaviors if you demonstrate them as part of your own behavior and express appreciation to your child when he behaves appropriately. Excusing rude behavior from your child because she doesn't know any better only teaches her that this behavior is acceptable.

The probability is that your youngster doesn't know any better, but she won't learn the right way if you don't teach it to her. Approach teaching her good table manners as you would teach any skill, and remember, it requires patience and practice.

LET MEALTIME BE AN OCCASION TO GROW CLOSER TO YOUR CHILD

Sitting down to eat together is a perfect occasion for parent and child to talk about feelings and experiences

—a time to raise questions, search for answers, discover hidden fears and joys, and learn how the family operates —skills a child will need as she moves into her own future. Turn off the TV, put down the newspaper, let the phone ring. You'll never reclaim the moment!

BIBLIOTHERAPY

Bread and Jam for Frances, by Russell Hoban
Cloudy with a Chance of Meatballs, by Judi Barrett
Eating Out, by Helen Oxenbury
Gregory, the Terrible Eater, by Mitchell Sharmat
Pancakes for Breakfast, by Tomie DePaola

FOLLOWING INSTRUCTIONS

"I'M COMING!"

Sound Familiar? *"How many times do I have to tell you . . ."*

You told your four-year-old that it's time to clean up his toys. Head bowed over his building blocks, he doesn't even look up when he defiantly states, "I don't want to." A little firmer this time, you demand, "Clean up your toys right this minute." Your precious preschooler throws himself on the floor kicking and screaming and cries out, "I want to play. I don't want to clean up!"

The Tune Your Child Sings: *"But I'm having fun."*

Your child doesn't want to give up the pleasure of what he's doing at the moment for the unknown. He can't understand your sense of urgency and thinks that if he complains loudly enough, you'll change your mind.

Low Notes: *"Do it now, or else."*

Incensed by your son's outright defiance, you head toward him, grab him by the shoulders, and look him straight in the eye. "You have no reason to be angry. If you don't start putting your toys away, Mommy will have to spank you." You leave the room before you raise a hand, and five minutes later you return to the scene.

Exasperated that your child hasn't moved, *you* start putting the colored building pieces away.

Stop! Rewind Your Own Tape: *"I'll be there in a minute."*

Take a minute to think about how you feel when someone interrupts you. Imagine how you'd react if you were comfortably curled up in your favorite chair reading a book and your spouse bounded into the room saying, "Hey, honey, will you come help me in the yard?" Irked that your mate would have the nerve to interrupt your momentary vacation, you brush him off with "I'll be with you in a couple of minutes. I just want to finish this chapter." What you've done is asked for some transition time—to get out of one mode and into another.

High Notes: *Transitioning is key.*

When you want to transition your child from one activity to another—especially from something he's enjoying to something you need him to do—prepare him for the change that is about to occur. When you know you'll want your child to clean up his room soon, poke your head in his room and say, "Sweetie, in five minutes you'll need to clean up your toys." Sometimes that warning is enough to ease your child into compliance when you return after countdown.

If your little one still isn't ready to comply, let him know you understand. "Honey, I know it's hard to st~~op~~ playing when you're having so much fun, but ~~it's~~ go." To make the news easier to swallo~~w~~ assistance. "I'll pick up the blue pieces w~~hile you pick~~ up the red ones." Even try making a race can get his color picked up first. Or offer an incentive such as "If you can get your toys put away, you'll have time for me to read you a book."

When the task is finally accomplished, show your appreciation—even if you had to use all the parenting tactics you could muster to accomplish the feat.

Are adults' clocks set faster than children's, or do kids just lack any sense of time? What can you do to make your child have the same sense of urgency as you do? How can you get him to stop fooling around and start paying attention? What's it going to take to make her follow instructions?

You may not be able to program your child to move in fast forward, but you can stop *demanding* he do things and discover these new tools to spur him along.

PREPARE KIDS FOR A CHANGE IN THE SPEED LIMIT

Children don't operate on adult time. Their world is much simpler than that. To expect them to react to the need for speed is like expecting an elephant to run a four-minute mile—it ain't gonna happen. The way to get your little one moving is to help her anticipate and prepare for the change in attitude and altitude. Certainly, in an emergency situation you are going to take over and carry her along kicking and screaming, but under ordinary circumstances, a little forewarning about a change goes a long way toward keeping parent and child in harmony.

USE A TIMER TO MEASURE AND MOTIVATE SUCCESS

If a fire alarm sounded, chances are you'd vacate the premises in no time flat. That's because you have the physical and mental maturity to respond immediately. Unfortunately, kids don't. If you were a child who heard the alarm, you'd have to go through a number of separate mental exercises before you processed the information and could make a decision about what to do. First you'd have to become aware of the bell. Then you would have to understand what it represented. Finally you would have to react to it and take action. These steps can be applied across the board to children's reactions to change.

Prepare your child for change. For example, when you know your child will need to clean up, get ready for bed, come to the dinner table, or get ready to leave the house, set a timer indicating the amount of time she has remaining to finish what she's doing. Then tell her, "When the bell goes off it will mean that it's time to stop watching TV and get your jacket to leave." This allows your child time to transition her thinking from what she is doing to what she *will* be doing. If an alarm clock or timer isn't available, a verbal reminder that something is about to happen will work. Investing a little time up front goes a long way in making the transition easier on everyone.

MAKE SURE YOUR CHILD HAS HEARD YOU AND UNDERSTANDS WHAT YOU'VE SAID

When talking to children, make sure you're at eye level and you actually have their attention. Many times, a parent will give her youngster a direction and assume that it's been heard and understood. Then, when the child has not done as asked, the parent is angry. But children can have selective hearing, and if they're enjoying what they're doing, stopping to comply with your needs is not necessarily on their agenda.

After you've given instructions, don't hesitate to ask your child to repeat your words: "Honey, what do I need you to do in five minutes?" If she gives you the right answer, thank her for listening.

INTERRUPT THE DISTRACTION RATHER THAN EXPECT YOUR CHILD TO TURN AWAY FROM IT

When selective listening reigns, it's often easier to physically stop your child in the middle of an activity than to keep repeating your warning or instructions. Without anger, turn off the TV, ask for the video joystick, take away the toy car, etc. Then, even though your child might be indignant and protest, look him in the eyes and repeat the instructions in a calm manner. If the protests continue and you know your child has heard and understood your request, don't keep telling him what to do. Just simply ask, "What did I say?" Use that phrase in a nonhostile way every time your child raises a new excuse or protest. In most cases, you'll wear him down until he finally complies. If a tantrum ensues, physically carry or lead your child by the hand to the destination. If that means you have to move him into your car and forfeit toothbrushing or hair combing, do it.

BE CLEAR WITH YOUR INSTRUCTIONS AND DON'T OVERWHELM

As a parent, it's your responsibility to make sure your child understands your request and that you don't expect more from her than she's capable of doing at her age and maturity level. Avoid making instructions so vague that they leave a wide latitude for interpretation. "Clean up your room" is a biggy. Maybe you have a concept of what that means, but to your child it may mean nothing more than making her bed.

Conversely, don't give too many instructions at one time and assume that they register with your child. "Make your bed, put your dirty clothes in the hamper, hang up your clean clothes, put your toys and books on their shelves . . . now!" is overwhelming to a kid. He is still processing *make your bed* while you've moved on to *clothes in the hamper*. And is it fair that he gets in trouble for not doing everything you asked, when he can barely remember the first request?

To avoid this scenario, after you give your child instructions, ask him what's expected of him. While you may consider this coddling, it's important always to keep in mind that a young child's memory is nowhere near the level of a mature adult's. Besides, this kind of active feedback is used frequently in a business setting to make sure wires don't get crossed when one person gives instructions to another. It just makes good sense.

BECOME A BROKEN RECORD

Children have an uncanny ability to so derail a discussion that parents barely remember the issue at hand and kids walk away scot-free. Instead of getting into a verbal sparring, practice the broken-record manner of gaining cooperation from children. Just keep repeating what you want in a calm tone. Eventually, when they see they aren't getting their way, they'll give up.

Remember, children don't have to like your requests. Storming off, slamming doors, and screaming childish epitaphs such as "I hate you" is typical childlike behavior. Kids really don't mean it. What they mean is "I hate the power you have over me to make me do what you want regardless of what I want." Or they may be trying to say, "I hate being small in the land of people who are all bigger than I am."

When your child sends verbal barbs, acknowledge her feelings, but don't get sucked into the emotions. Rather than yelling back, "Don't you ever say you hate me!" try saying, "I know you're angry right now." That's tough to do, but it's not worth another hassle between the two of you at a moment when your child is already thinking and acting irrationally.

AVOID COMPARING YOUR ACTIVE, CURIOUS CHILD TO A DOCILE, COMPLIANT ONE

Children, as a rule, want to please their parents, but sometimes parents make that almost impossible. They set up hard-to-achieve standards, communicate expectations poorly, and then punish the child for not being successful. One tactic parents fall into is comparing a child who is not behaving at the parent's behest to another child who is. Each child is unique. Expecting one to behave at the same ability level as another again sets up a system of failure.

Imagine having dinner at the home of someone who is an excellent cook, while you have trouble making toast without burning it. How would it feel if your spouse said to you, "Gee, wouldn't it be great if you could make meat loaf as good as this!" Rather than thinking, Oh yeah, I can't wait to go home and try this recipe, you think, Fat chance of my meat loaf ever tasting like this. And then, you NEVER MAKE MEAT LOAF AGAIN!

Children experience the same sense of shame and guilt when compared to other kids. Rather than the comparison being a motivator for better behavior, it becomes an inhibitor of positive change. Much more effective is establishing behavior standards for each of your children based on careful consideration of his or her unique abilities. Of course, you will run into the "How come you never yell at her for doing what you just yelled at me for?" But don't get sucked into the "You love her more than you love me" gambit children will use to rip at your heart and get you to bend to their wishes. Instead, stay focused on the issue. Don't get swayed, no matter what the urging of the injured party. You might say, "I'm not talking to her right now, I'm talking to you. What I expect from you is based on what *you* can do and not what she can do. This is not an issue about love."

Your child, artful manipulator that he is, will try to wear you down, but remain strong. "That's not fair!" is the battle cry of children who don't have the ability to fight with verbal acuity. Instead, respond with "You're right. Life isn't fair, but that's what makes it so interesting." Then reiterate whatever it is you want done.

CONSIDER THE CIRCUMSTANCES FROM YOUR CHILD'S PERSPECTIVE

There is a part of every parent that believes that children should take total responsibility for their actions. Imagine you've just declared your child's play area a national disaster and you want her to clean it all up. You tell her in just so many words what you expect. Your child, however, surveys the room and feels overwhelmed by the task. She becomes incapable of moving to action because she doesn't know where to begin. Instead of being angry, understand that to this little child you are asking her to clean up after the Mount Saint Helens eruption. Frankly, she sees her job as making messes, not tidying them up.

Instead of demanding compliance, consider the issue from another perspective. The last time Thanksgiving dinner was at your house and twenty-four family members and friends joined in for the festivities, what did the house look like after everybody went home? Did you jump right in and clean up or did you: (1) consider the tasks at hand, (2) break them into small, doable jobs, (3) ask for help from others, and (4) reward yourself each time another little piece of the mess was removed?

Children should be entitled to the same privilege of breaking a big job into smaller pieces. As the parent, you should help your child dissect the big job into smaller tasks as a means of teaching her how to tackle problems. And remember, it's not inappropriate to assist your child in his tasks even though you didn't make the mess. We all appreciate a helping hand.

SET UP YOUR CHILD'S ENVIRONMENT TO MINIMIZE DISASTERS

One way to minimize the disasters your child is capable of creating is to set up an environment and rules that place limits on his behavior. Here are a few suggestions:

- Have available to little hands only a few toys that are easily manageable even when all of them are played with at the same time.
- Remind your child about the rule that says one toy goes back in its storage place before he takes another one.
- Make sure there is ample storage space and that the child is capable of returning the toys to their appropriate place.

REMEMBER THE BIG PICTURE

Children are young for such a short period of time that putting on an angry face for all of the little infractions sets up a pattern of negative reinforcement. You don't want to spend time that should be cherished and enjoyed solely focusing on enforcing rules and regulations. Make your rules wisely. Stick to them. But don't be so intent on making things perfect that you can't overlook the toy sticking out of the toy box or the shoes hiding under the bed. Give kids a break. They are, after all, only young once.

CREATE A CLIMATE OF ENJOYABLE FAMILY SUPPORT

Rather than saying to your child, "Clean up this mess right now," you might say, "You put all of the trucks and cars in their basket and I'll put all of the people and blocks in their boxes. Let's see who can get their job done faster." Now it's a game and not a punishment. In no time the task will be finished and you and your child will have shared a good time. Otherwise, the time shared will become nothing but a battle of wills and no one wins, even if you won a blue ribbon.

SHOW YOUR APPRECIATION WHEN YOUR CHILD COMPLIES

When your child does what you ask, even if you had to fight her every step of the way, thank her for her cooperation. This reinforces your expectations and shows her what she can do to earn your appreciation. Children typically will behave as you ask if they can expect a positive response from you.

These little bundles of joy and energy come into this world believing the universe revolves around them. They respond to the demands of living with others as if they were royalty, expecting others to do their bidding. It is only with loving guidance and patience from you that they'll begin to understand that the world revolves around a community and not its individuals. It is only then that they'll begin to change their behavior. But be patient. Such change happens slowly, over time. But rest assured it will happen. It's part of the process of developing from child to adult. You just can't rush it, no matter how much you try.

BIBLIOTHERAPY

Disobeying, by Joy Wilt Berry
Strega Nona, by Tomie DePaola
The Grouchy Ladybug, by Eric Carle
Where the Wild Things Are, by Maurice Sendak
Eggbert, by Tom Ross and Rex Barron

GOING PLACES

"I PROMISE I'LL BE GOOD."

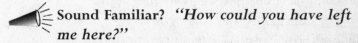 **Sound Familiar?** *"How could you have left me here?"*

As you walk into the studio to pick up your four-year-old daughter from her ballet lesson, the teacher comments, "Your little Tyler is so-o-o well behaved." You turn to see whom she's talking to and realize there's no one else around. You ask yourself, "It couldn't be my child she's describing, could it?" Then, as Tyler stomps toward you and throws her ballet slippers at your knees, it dawns on you that the Tyler the ballet teacher sees and the one you live with are not one and the same. . . .

The Tune Your Child Sings: *"I was so afraid you wouldn't come back for me."*

While your child may love ballet lessons, preschool, or Grandma's house, kids are still scared when Mom and Dad leave them. The biggest fear young children have is the fear of abandonment. Even though kids seem headstrong and independent at times, they are, in reality, totally reliant on their parents to provide safety and security. When left for extended periods of time without parental security, children can't help but wonder if Mom or Dad is really going to remember to come back.

So why, if your kid loves you so much, doesn't she show it by welcoming you with a big smile and warm

75

hug? Why on earth would Tyler throw her ballet slippers at the one person she loves more than anyone else in the world? After a separation, returning to the safety of parents is such a relief that the pent-up tension of worrying if Mom would return and the stress of having to be on her best behavior for her teacher comes pouring out in tears, tantrums, and aggression.

Low Notes: *"I'm so embarrassed."* You can't believe your own flesh and blood would throw her shoes at you. With the teacher standing there and other parents coming to pick up their kids, you try to ignore her deviant behavior. You chuckle to hide your indignation, and rather than reprimand her, you pick up the ballet shoes, grab her hand, and try to slink out of the studio. All the while your "well-behaved" darling screams, "Don't pull me! You're hurting my arm!"

Stop! Rewind Your Own Tape: *The Girdle Syndrome.*
Your child lashing out at the one she loves is not much different from the spouse who bites his tongue all day long at the injustices he feels at work and releases the unexpressed irritations on an unsuspecting spouse at home.

Ah, the Girdle Syndrome. You stuff yourself in and look great—on the outside. But as soon as you whip off the girdle in the privacy of your home, everything comes spilling out. When we wear an emotional girdle all day, pent-up frustration and anxiety can't help but pour out once we're safe and secure with those we love. Out in the world, we have to make a good impression—just as kids often try to do when at school or staying with relatives.

High Notes: *"I'll always be there for you."* While you don't want your child to act pouty, you needn't be angry at her for releasing her emotions. Empathy for how she's feeling ("I know it's been a long lesson") and a show of joy at being reunited ("But I'm so glad we're together again") should calm the stress of separation.

Even though you might like to change roles with the teacher who dubbed your daughter "so well behaved," remember that your child wouldn't be acting out if there weren't a bond between you. As crazy as it sounds, when your child misbehaves after a separation, it's just her way of saying, "I love you, and I know you love me."

Often parents heighten the emotions of separation when arriving to pick up their child by talking to the adult in charge and ignoring their little one. While you need an update on how your child behaved, always take time first to acknowledge her: "I missed you. I'm so happy to see you." That recognition will negate the need for your youngster to try to get your attention in an unacceptable manner.

One of the gifts children often lay at their parents' feet is acting wonderful away from home and then turning into recognizable monsters when back in the comfort of immediate family. That means they are learning the rules of social behavior their parents have tried so hard to instill and are applying them to the outside world. Their

Dr. Jekyll and Mr. Hyde routines demonstrate they know they are loved unconditionally at home, and don't have to behave perfectly just for Mom and Dad!

It should afford you some solace that you're not the only parents whose child either turns into a little devil at just the moment you need her to behave her best or behaves perfectly for others and then releases pent-up emotions in the safe harbor of home. Not many parents today adhere to the tenet "Kids will be kids." Instead, we expect our four- and six-year-olds to act like little adults. We forget how keyed up special events can make them and how tired they get when they're out and about, away from their regular routine.

Follow these suggestions to achieve the kind of behavior you desire from your child when you're on the go with him or have to leave him in the care of another:

UNDERSTAND HOW YOUR CHILDREN FEEL WHEN YOU ARE AWAY FROM THEM

Children are 100 percent dependent on their parents to meet their every need—from food, clothing, shelter, and companionship to transportation, guidance, and discipline. When you're apart—even if it's because of a daily routine like work—your child's immature emotional makeup causes him to believe that maybe this time you won't come back.

One of the scariest notions children face is that they'll be left to care for themselves in a world of strangers. Imagine attending a sold-out concert with your best friend whom you entrusted to be the keeper of the money, car keys, and identification, and the two of you become separated. As a reasoning adult, you know that eventually you will find your friend. But as a living, breathing, feeling human being, a part of you is frightened. You worry about how you'll get to eat and get home, and what would happen if you got hurt and had no ID. That's scary stuff for an adult. Now, just think how a child feels when his life support is taken away.

The fear of abandonment causes kids to act out unmercifully. Children react to their world at skin level; they express their fears and joys with gay abandon. They don't consider or care how others (including you) will react to their behavior; they just do it. In fact, they don't yet have the capacity to actually contemplate how they'll react—self-monitoring of behaviors and responses comes with age. Children's behaviors are not planned. They just are.

PREPARE YOUR CHILD FOR A SEPARATION

Even if telling your child you'll be leaving him with a caregiver brings on tears and tantrums, it's better to prepare a child than to surprise him. He'll learn how to cope when things don't go his way by having had coping experiences *and* the assurance from you that he'll be all right.

Let your child know how long you'll be gone and where you'll be while you're apart. If it helps your child feel better, give him something familiar to hold while you're gone. That might be his blankie, your hankie, or whatever it takes to gain a sense of control. Tell your child that crying because he is sad is okay, and the adult in charge will help him feel better. At the same time, remind your little guy that you have all the confidence in the world that he'll do just fine while you're gone and that you look forward to reconnecting when you return.

If you always leave your child to go to a specific place, such as your work site, set aside some time one day to take your child there to see it. That will give him an image of where you are when you're not together. For long periods of separation, pictures and audio- or video-tapes can be a wonderful bridge between the leaving and the returning. While these crutches may seem to perpetuate infancy, they actually help children grapple with the ever-changing complexities of their lives.

If your child has trouble in new environments, give him an opportunity to warm up to a new place *before* you leave. Or leave him for only short periods of time before you depart for an extended period of time. Showing your child this kind of respect when he is little will help him go courageously into the world when he has much more freedom.

MAKE SURE YOUR CHILD KNOWS THE KIND OF BEHAVIOR EXPECTED AND ACCEPTED WHEN SHE'S AWAY FROM YOU AND IN THE CARE OF ANOTHER

Remind your child that you expect her to remember good manners and use "magic" words like *please* and *thank you*. If you don't think your child has the skills necessary to get along on her own, unprompted by you, practice. Set up times when you can rehearse how your child should behave when you're away. This might mean leaving her with a neighbor for a half hour while you're right next door. That way, future experiences when you're away farther and longer will not be as harrowing.

Your child will likely behave according to your expectations. If you expect her to get in trouble, she probably will. But if you expect her to be competent and capable, she'll want to show you that your faith in her is well placed. When you hear that your child has behaved as expected, reward her with hugs and kisses and warm words of love.

HOLD PRACTICE SESSIONS TO TEACH CHILDREN HOW TO BEHAVE IN SOCIAL SETTINGS

It's asking too much to think that your child has all the social skills of an adult. In fact, there are adults who don't know how to act in certain social settings. When commoners are to be introduced to royalty, they receive specific instructions on how to talk, bow or curtsy, and shake hands. Nothing is left to the imagination. There is a protocol, and you learn it only by having it explained to you and then practicing.

Do the same with your child. If you are going to Aunt May's, explain that she may see a lot of knickknacks that may be looked at but not touched. Then foreshadow the events so she knows what will happen: "We are going to visit for a little while in the living room, then we'll eat dinner"—(teach her that there is a meat called pot roast)—"and after dessert, we'll all go for a walk down to the recreation center and listen to some music."

LET OTHER ADULT CAREGIVERS KNOW HOW TO RESPOND TO YOUR CHILD IF HE SHOULD ACT OUT WHEN YOU'RE NOT AROUND

Communicating what is typical of your child is critically important when leaving him with others. If your child is supersensitive and falls apart easily, advise the adult in charge of what to expect and how to respond. If your child is so stoic he won't ask for help, make sure this information is also passed along.

Along with telling the adult caregiver what to expect from your child, let your child know what to expect from the caregiver. Remind him that while the adult in charge will not act the same as his parents, the caregiver should not hit or physically hurt him. Don't assume your child is safe and respected. When you're home, ask your child how things went and encourage him to talk about how the caregiver acted. When your child knows you're listening, he's more likely to reveal untoward behavior.

MAKE REUNIONS SPECIAL

When you arrive to pick up your child, show him how happy you are to see him again. Your child missed you and assumes you missed him. So, if you walk in and begin talking to the adult in charge, your child may question your love and loyalty. When kids feel ignored, they'll do anything TO GET YOUR ATTENTION, including tugging, screaming, or acting out with others to make you notice them. Any good behavior they exhibited while you were away will be wiped out in one minute of stress and frustration.

Take a few minutes when you reconnect to pay attention to your child. Children need constant reassurance that they are lovable and loved. Don't you? Just think how great you feel when your spouse, unsolicited, says, "I love you and I'm glad you're a part of my life." You know intellectually that you're loved, but hearing it and seeing it demonstrated in little ways are still important. This is no less true for children. Once they are recognized with love when you return, they'll probably afford you a little time to talk to the adult, be it a friend who baby-sat, or a teacher, coach, dance instructor, etc.

But if things don't go well and your child falls apart upon your return, try not to overreact. Understand that children have a natural tendency to do whatever it takes to become emotionally balanced. They don't understand what they're doing, but if they feel stressed, they must "de-stress." That might mean tears, tantrums, fists against your chest, or toys flung across the floor. (Have you ever pounded on a table or slammed a door to release frustration?)

If you respond with anger, their stress increases. They don't understand that you're reacting to their behavior. They just know they're feeling lonely and scared and they want you to hold them and love them. But instead, you're yelling.

SET AND ENFORCE LOVING CONSEQUENCES BEFORE A PROBLEM OCCURS

Whenever possible, tell your child up front what will happen if he misbehaves. That way there are no surprises —for you or for him. If you've stated specific consequences, such as no TV tomorrow if he doesn't turn it off today when you ask, it will help you to not fly off the handle and hand down punishments too big for the infraction. By setting the consequences ahead of time, if your child misbehaves he has actually chosen to receive the consequences. You laid out the scenario, and you're no longer the bad guy. The child had complete responsibility.

Don't let the emotions of the moment harm your long-term relationship with your child. While it's important to follow through with discipline, it's also paramount for kids to know that if things don't go as you expected, it is not the end of the world. They must be granted some room for error, and they need to know that if they make mistakes, it doesn't change your love for them.

TELL YOUR CHILD ALL THE WONDERFUL THINGS THAT WILL HAPPEN IF SHE MEETS YOUR EXPECTATIONS

Part of telling children what is expected is explaining the positive consequences of compliant behavior. Make statements such as "If you and your friend play nicely together while his mom and I are visiting, he can come over to our house on Saturday" or "If you follow instructions at your soccer practice, you will be able to go again." These kinds of statements reinforce positive behavior. While you have to let your child know what will happen if things don't go as planned, it accomplishes more when you phrase things in a positive light.

Whenever you set up positive consequences, make sure you follow through just as you would if she did something negative. Rewards for good behavior must be continually reinforced so children can see how much control they have over what happens to them.

DON'T TAKE YOUR CHILD'S PUBLIC MISBEHAVIOR SO PERSONALLY THAT YOU EMBARRASS HER

Most parents respond to a child's public display of anger with embarrassment and concern about what others are thinking of them and their parenting skills. But most other adults are thinking, Thank heaven that isn't me.

It doesn't matter what other people think. What happens between you and your child has to be based on what works for both of you, not on the expectations of others —who have NO IDEA about you or your family structure.

Because of what others might think, parents often embarrass, humiliate, or spank their kids. Trying to show some control, these parents get way out of control— much more than they would have had the infraction occurred in their own home. Putting down or punishing kids in public causes a sense of shame that can devastate them. It may also escalate their behavior rather than minimize it.

Understand that kids are not trying to humiliate adults. They don't think about the reactions of others because they don't react from an intellectual position. They respond from pure surface emotions. They are not being diabolical; they are only children learning how to get along in the world.

CONTROL YOURSELF THE MOST WHEN YOUR CHILD IS OUT OF CONTROL IN PUBLIC

When your child misbehaves for all to see, take a deep breath. Remind yourself that you're the adult and by virtue of that status, you're smarter and better able to control yourself than your child is. Show your child the same respect you'd want from your spouse. Take him aside and, talking quietly, let him know that his behavior is unacceptable. Give the little guy an opportunity to regain his composure before you expect him to correct his behavior. Telling a child to stop crying is like telling a puncture wound to stop bleeding. Bleeding is what it will do until it's ready to stop (with minor intervention on your part). The same principle applies to a child's tears. He will cry until he feels better.

If your child decides to throw a minor tantrum, let him. Tell him you'll wait patiently until he is done and then you can complete what you were out to do. When there is no payoff for a behavior, it usually stops. Walk away from him to a distance that is close enough for you to see each other but not to talk.

But telling your child to stop because you are embarrassed will have NO IMPACT! Just don't get sucked into the tantrum. It will run its course if you don't reward it with your attention. If the tantrum becomes a way for your child to engage you, you're teaching him how to get your attention. Sarah Bernhardt couldn't hold a candle to a child who's learned how to use a temper tantrum for his own gain.

If your child doesn't stop the tantrum and you must impose a consequence, get ready for your child to plead for a second chance. "I didn't mean it! It will never happen again!" At that moment, he means every word, but if you don't enforce your rules and follow through with the consequences, your child learns that groveling is a way out of any dilemma.

Let your son know you appreciate that he will do

better in the future, but that doesn't change the current situation. He behaved in a manner that earned the consequence, and it must be implemented. This type of response reinforces that the child should learn from the experience and make a concerted effort to change. But getting away with something by promising not to repeat the infraction will have an impact only until he finds himself in the exact same situation the next time.

BIBLIOTHERAPY

Don't Drag Your Feet, by Joseph Low
I Don't Want to Go, I Don't Know How to Act, by Robert M. Quackenbush
If Everybody Did, by JoAnn Stover
Hattie Be Quiet, Hattie Be Good, by Dick Gackenback
Will You Come Back for Me?, by Ann Tompert

HITTING, BITING, AND MAKING FACES

"I'M NOT YOUR FRIEND ANYMORE!"

Sound Familiar? *If looks could kill.*
You've just told your child not to eat in the living room, and he makes that face that speaks a thousand words. He sits there, pouting, with that "Make me stop!" kind of look. You repeat your command, but your child is now experiencing selective hearing, and continues to drop cookie crumbs on the carpet.

The Tune Your Child Sings: *"I'm angry at the power you have over me."*
If you could read your child's mind, he'd probably be thinking, I really don't like what you have to say. I'm angry at the power you have over me. Maybe if I make these faces you'll get angry or feel sorry for me and go away. Then I can eat my cookies in front of the TV.

Children often lack the verbal skills to express themselves. Instead, they resort to using their faces and bodies to communicate their feelings. They make faces or strike out and hit—sometimes even bite—because they don't have the ability to reason, arbitrate, or compromise.

Low Notes: *"Don't look at me like that!"*
You read the words behind the face your child makes and go ballistic. "Don't look at me like that!" you

command, your brow furrowed and your teeth clenched. "You know the rules about eating in the living room. Now give me that cookie and go to your room."

Stop! Rewind Your Own Tape: *What gesture did you make at the police officer?*
Remember the last time a police officer pulled you over for a traffic violation? After he wrote you the ticket and walked away, did you sit there and smile, or did you secretly dart evil looks at his backside and wish him four flat tires? Caught in an illegal act by an officer of the law, you felt powerless. You couldn't hit him. You couldn't vaporize him. And you couldn't tear the ticket into bite-sized pieces. Your only recourse was to get back at him with angry thoughts and devilish expressions. Yes, it was immature of you, but somehow it made you feel better —at least for a moment.

High Notes: *Little eyes are watching.*
Young kids don't understand the pain their be-havior can cause an adult. And lashing out at children when they act out their aggressions will not teach them how to get what they want in an appropriate manner. It's essential that parents watch their own facial expres-sions and body language when communicating with chil-dren. Rolling your eyes at their bothersome antics is hurtful to them, also. As much as possible, try to remain calm and *say* how you feel.

The next time your cookie monster makes a face at you, say, "I don't like it when you make faces at me. It hurts my feelings. You have a beautiful face and when you scrunch it up like that I don't like to look at it.

I'm leaving now. When you're ready to show me your beautiful face, I'll be happy to talk with you.''

Parents delight when their children make happy, joyous faces, but are offended and outraged by expressions of anger. In both cases, kids are communicating in the simplest way they know how.

Young children have limited resources to handle feelings of anger, and they lack the sophistication and capacity to consider other people's feelings. They use their bodies to express their emotions because they don't have the words to tell somebody how they're feeling. If you're thwarting their attempt to get what they want, they can't say, "Excuse me, Dad, I don't want to eat any more of my peas, and frankly, I want them off my plate now." Instead, they throw their peas on the floor and cry.

Similarly, when children see somebody playing with something they desire, they might use their teeth as a form of oral communication to get what they want. They don't do this to hurt the other child or to make you angry. Their behavior is based solely on their needs and wants with no regard for anyone else. When a young child bites another child, that action doesn't have the same import to him as it does to the adults in their lives. By a child's definition, what's been bitten is not a person but an obstacle in his way. Understanding feelings and acts of recrimination are *not* part of a child's language skills.

For you to strike out with words or hand when your child expresses his feelings with his body is contradictory to the behavior change you hope to achieve. Your child looks to you to be a rational force in his life. If you're out of control, what the heck is he supposed to do?

The following suggestions will help you teach your

child how to communicate appropriately, without re-
sorting to physical violence or hurtful expressions.

RECOGNIZE THAT CHILDREN HAVE REASONS FOR GETTING ANGRY

Children are human, and just like adults, they get angry.
They resent the fact that they are powerless over their
own lives. Everyone, including older siblings, tells them
what to do. And young children, unique and incredible
beings that they are, have their own agenda, which is
often in direct conflict with what everyone else wants.
Since behavior is their main means of communication,
what better way to tell you they're tired, hungry, sad,
or sick than falling apart on the floor or throwing a ball
at your new vase.

How your child behaves has nothing to do with you
and everything to do with him. Try not to internalize his
actions. That doesn't mean you should allow disrespectful behavior. Educate him about what is acceptable and
what is not in a way that teaches but doesn't condemn.

ACCEPT THAT CHILDREN DON'T ALWAYS KNOW WHAT THEY WANT

Kids fuss and fight because they want a particular toy
and when they get it, they cry because they now want
something else. These aberrations are just children learning to function in a world that offers many pleasures but
then allows them to choose only a few. Sometimes kids
don't know what they want, and face it, at times adults
don't either. What looks awful today might be the key
to contentment tomorrow. If their behavior isn't hurting
anybody, give your children the opportunity to express
themselves. Remember, it does us all good to rant and

rave a little, and sometimes just venting frustration makes things better.

KEEP IN MIND THAT CHILDREN DO NOT UNDERSTAND THE "WHY" OF THINGS

Asking your child "Why did you do that?" will net you only an "I don't know" or a shoulder shrug. And although you want to know what makes that little mind tick, don't get onto that frustrating merry-go-round. Instead, point out what happened and how she could have dealt with the situation. "Hurting your friend is not the way to get him to give up a toy so you can play with it. Sometimes you just have to wait your turn. Would you like to play with the car while Jimmy finishes playing with the horse?" A little distraction goes a long way to change a potentially explosive situation. But if your child is belligerent and says, "No, I want the car now!" reinforce that he will have to wait, or make suggestions such as "Why don't you take turns? Each of you can play with a toy for five minutes and then you must give someone else a turn. Would you like me to set the timer?"

TELL YOUR CHILD HOW SHE CAN GET YOUR ATTENTION IN A MORE POSITIVE WAY

Whenever possible, try to teach your little one lessons from a child's perspective. Tell her that her behavior or words have hurt your feelings. Let her know you don't like it and will not react or respond to it. Then let her know what she can do to get your attention. "When you want Mommy to help you get your snuggie bear down from the shelf, you can ask, 'Mommy, can you get my bear for me?' " If whining is a problem, try saying, "I can't hear you when you whine. If you want something, use your words in your big-girl voice so I can understand you. If you don't, I can't help you."

WITHDRAW ATTENTION FROM YOUR CHILD UNTIL SHE COMPLIES AND BEHAVES IN AN APPROPRIATE MANNER

What children want more than anything is their parents' attention. Take that away, and kids quickly modify their behavior to get their parents to notice them again. At times, it's the better part of valor to ignore your child. If your daughter is annoying you but not hurting anybody or anything, you might choose not to reward her annoying behavior with your attention. It's hard not to yell at her to stop, but if you can maintain your composure and continue with whatever you're doing, she'll learn this is one way that certainly won't gain her favor.

When your child is acting out, ask her to stop in a polite way or tell her your expectations: "When you stop pouting, I will continue playing the game with you" or "You can watch TV again, just as soon as you put your crayons away and wipe that scowl off your face." Though it's hard for adults to understand, if you get angry, your child has still won your attention and kept you engaged. Though you might be seething inside, keep a calm veneer on the outside.

Then, as soon as your child behaves appropriately, thank her and continue what you were doing. This will reinforce desired behaviors.

REMOVE YOUR CHILD FROM A STRESSFUL SITUATION

When your child has lost control of a situation, getting angry because he's angry won't help your child regain his composure. Instead, remove your child from the inciting incident. This time-out is not a punishment. It's a time away from stimulation which provides the child with an opportunity to pull himself together. It's much like a sports team taking a time-out off the field because they're not doing too well. They need a chance to restrategize and reorganize.

There are many ways to handle this separation. You might remove the child and ask him to sit quietly for a few minutes. Or you might let him read a book or listen to quiet music for a moment to regain composure. Then, depending on his age, either ask him or tell him what happened to give him information from which to draw the next time he finds himself in a similar situation.

DON'T EXPECT CHILDREN TO LIKE BEING REMOVED FROM THE ACTION

Just as you don't like leaving a fun gathering with friends because you have to get to bed at a reasonable hour in order to function at work, your child doesn't like being separated from his friends or family members—even if he isn't getting along with them. Driving home from the party, you probably complain the whole time or wish you were independently wealthy and didn't have to go to work to earn a living. Let kids vent, too.

HELP YOUR CHILD UNDERSTAND HOW HIS ANGRY BEHAVIOR MAKES OTHERS FEEL

Allowing your child to be rude and disrespectful or to hurt others doesn't teach him to value other people's feelings. When your child hurts someone else, with either words or physical actions, help him learn from his mistakes in a way he can understand. That means approaching the situation from your child's perspective, and *doesn't* include hitting a child for hitting or biting a child for biting. Those actions teach a child that hitting and biting are acceptable behaviors. Instead, try to get a child to think in terms of how he'd feel if what he did had been done to him.

While some children are born with an innate sense of caring and awareness of other's feelings, some children need to have it demonstrated. "How do you think Grandma felt when you called her 'dummy'? Do you think it would be all right if she called you 'dummy'? How do you think it would feel for someone to call you 'dummy'? You made Grandma feel bad when you called her a name. What can you do to make her feel better?"

All of these questions help children begin to connect their actions to the rest of the world. Anger and punishment won't expand their base of knowledge to allow for a change in their behavior. Anger only teaches them angry and hostile behavior. If you consider that the role of the parent is to guide children to functioning at a higher level in the real world, teaching children to be empathetic will make more sense. It's easier to get angry and lash out because it's a natural response, but it won't accomplish your goal.

EXAMINE THE ROLE MODELS IN YOUR CHILD'S LIFE

If you aren't satisfied with your child's behavior toward others, take a close look at the people in her life whom she imitates. If children are exposed to rudeness, they will repeat it.

EVALUATE HOW YOU AND YOUR SPOUSE TREAT EACH OTHER

Does your child learn the art of making nasty faces from watching her parents interact with each other? Are you an eye roller, a "stick-out-your-tongue" revenge artist, or better yet, quick to "flip off" that idiot in the next lane even when your youngster is in the car? Children cannot discriminate good behavior from bad. All the behavior they're exposed to is fair game for repetition.

DON'T LET "TV KIDS" TEACH YOUR KIDS HOW TO ACT

Children portrayed on television are notorious for being disrespectful toward their parents specifically and other adults in general. But the laugh track rewards their behavior. If children view disrespectful behavior as a means of getting noticed, they will repeat what they see.

When you're watching television with your child and you see an example of good or bad behavior, comment on it. "Did you hear what that child said to his grandmother? We don't talk like that; it's rude." Or "It is not funny to talk to your mother and father that way. If *you* talk like that, you will find that rather than getting noticed you will be asked to go to your room." Or "Did you notice how that little boy asked his father if he would please help him build a kite? That's one good way to get Mommy or Daddy to listen to you and want to help." Your child will get the message if you use television as a tool for teaching behaviors that are expected and acceptable rather than allowing it to seep into her subconscious without modulation by you.

ASK YOURSELF IF YOUR CHILD IS ACTING OUT AS A WAY OF ASKING FOR ATTENTION

Is your child's annoying behavior a plea for you to notice her? If you think the answer might be yes, don't ignore her or ask her to wait until you're ready to interact. Stop what you're doing, get down to her level, and give her a little bit of loving. That's another way to minimize those little behaviors that have the power to make you nuts.

Children are little and needy for such a short time. You might find that if you ignore your child when she's small and needs you, she might ignore you when you're the one in need of her attention. You don't want to wake up one day with regrets.

Consider this poem written by an unknown author:

One hundred years from now, it will not matter how
  clean my house was,
What kind of clothes I wore, or the car I drove.
It will not matter how much money I had in the bank.
What will matter is the impact I had on the life of a
  child.

BIBLIOTHERAPY

Alexander and the Terrible, Horrible, No Good, Very Bad Day, by
  Judith Viorst
Dinah's Mad, Bad Wishes, by Barbara M. Joosse
Even If I Did Something Awful?, by Barbara Shook Hazen
Making Faces, by Nick Butterworth
The Sorely Trying Day, by Russell Hoban

INDEPENDENCE

"I'd Rather Do It Myself."

◀≣ Sound Familiar? *"I can do it."*

You've got five minutes before the 8 A.M. car pool arrives. Your daughter wants to put on and tie her own tennis shoes. Although she's just turned four, she lacks the physical dexterity to accomplish the task. The minutes tick by and she is no closer to putting on her shoes than when she started ten minutes ago. You plead to help, but now she is angry and frustrated and so are you.

The Tune Your Child Sings: *"I'm a big girl."*

Your daughter has watched you put her shoes on her hundreds of times. Now she wants to do it herself. It looks simple, but she doesn't understand all that's involved. She has no concept of time or speed, and is moving so-o-o-o slowly. She isn't thinking about the others in the car pool, who will get to preschool late if she's not ready—nor about the mother who's driving and has to be at a meeting at 8:30 sharp.

When you intervene and try to do the task yourself, she feels that you don't think she's a big girl. Saying, "Hurry up" only makes her upset and doesn't help her get the shoes on any faster.

Low Notes: *Taking control.*

The clock chimes eight o'clock. Exasperated, you say, "Here, let me do it." But your child's only thanks for your loving assistance is a resounding "NO-O-O-O! I want to do it!"

The car pool pulls up in your driveway and honks the horn. You rip the shoe out of your daughter's hand and shove both of them on her feet, yelling that she's making everyone late. Your daughter breaks down in tears, and you break out in a cold sweat. You don't like yourself when you act like this, but what is a once-sane parent to do?

Stop! Rewind Your Own Tape: *"Don't plant my garden."*

Think how you'd feel if, in the middle of planting your first vegetable garden, your sister-in-law with a green thumb arrives. Amazed by your incompetence, she takes over. Her lack of respect and inability to let you practice new skills firsthand makes you feel incompetent. Children feel the same way when parents usurp their independence.

High Notes: *"We'll set up a time to practice after school."*

At 7:45 A.M., when your child tells you she wants to put on her shoes herself, you agree that she can try for several minutes. You tell her that five minutes before the car pool is to arrive, you'll need to help her so the others won't have to wait. When the appointed time comes, you gently take over. "Honey, let Mommy help now, the car pool is almost here." "No!" she cries. Keeping calm, you explain, "There is not enough time right now for you to put your shoes on by yourself. But we'll have time for you to practice after school." You firmly take the shoe, and as she resists, you repeat, "I know you want to put on your own shoes. You'll be able to practice after school today. I can't wait to help you learn how to do it!"

That evening, you set up a practice session. You show her how to loosen the laces, how to pull up the tongue of the shoe, and finally how to tie the laces. Step by step, you praise your child for her accomplishments, build her confidence, and demonstrate your interest in her success. Though it will take days, even weeks before she can accomplish the task solo, you keep enforcing the rule that at five minutes before eight o'clock, you must help her tie her shoes.

After reaching some degree of physical and mental maturity, your child is ready to explore the world on her own. She wants to feed herself, dress herself, answer the phone and the door, and, if she thought she could get away with it, drive the car.

Here are some ideas on how to foster independence yet maintain control, without damaging self-esteem.

BE AWARE OF THE SUBTLE MESSAGES YOU SEND WHEN YOU TRY TO TAKE OVER FOR YOUR CHILD

"I'd rather do it myself" is a common refrain heard around the world, from the developing child to the competent adult. That's because each success we achieve is an affirmation of our abilities. One of the biggest inhibitors of self-esteem is subtle messages parents send through tone of voice or body language that their children are not capable and competent. Kids take those kinds of messages to heart, and they impact children's willingness to go courageously into the world. When children attempt to do things that they may not have the developmental ability to do, refrain from taking over in a powerful way and, instead, offer assistance and wait for a response.

WEIGH YOUR CHILD'S NEED FOR INDEPENDENCE AGAINST YOUR NEED TO GET GOING

Children's cognitive development often expands faster than their physical ability. Short, fat fingers do not do much for many of the skills little ones want to attempt. When a child is thwarted by her own inability, you can anticipate a tantrum of frustration. When you intervene, which confirms her lack of competency, the tantrum escalates because she can now blame you and not take ownership and responsibility.

What happens here becomes a battle of needs. The child has needs to practice new skills and be successful. The parent has needs that are based on time. Whose needs should win in this scenario is not a simple "you or her." When time is truly a critical issue, the parent must intercede. It's not reasonable to be late to work or to hold up the entire family while a little one attempts an activity she's not yet capable of performing. However, constantly sending the message to your child that your needs always take precedence over hers is not fair, either.

IF THERE'S NO TIME TO ALLOW THE CHILD TO EXPERIMENT ON HIS OWN, AT LEAST ACKNOWLEDGE HIS ANGER

Sometimes, just recognizing a child's feelings is all that's necessary to avert a major confrontation. "I know you want to do this by yourself, but we just don't have the time today. I'm going to do it for you now, and we'll try again tomorrow by leaving some extra time before we must go." These little statements show your child that you respect him and accept that his needs and wants have value. It's these messages that say to a child, "I believe in you and your abilities." Receiving that message confirms the child's positive sense of self.

WHEN THE TIME COMES TO ASSIST, APPROACH YOUR CHILD FROM A POSITION OF SUPPORT, NOT ANGER

"I knew you couldn't get dressed by yourself, now I'll have to help you" is a lot different from "Hey, nice job. You were able to put on your undies and shorts. Now we'll just have to finish with your shirt and sandals. Tomorrow we'll start a little earlier because I know with a few more times of trying, you'll be able to do it all by yourself."

Parents may think that offering this kind of feedback takes a lot of work, especially when what they really want is just to get the task done. But it's an investment in your child's sense of self that will pay big dividends in years to come—when you want your child to have the confidence to try new things and take risks.

WHEN YOU MUST INTERCEDE, SPECIFICALLY STATE WHAT MUST HAPPEN AND HOW YOUR CHILD WILL HAVE ANOTHER OPPORTUNITY TO BE SUCCESSFUL LATER

Expect your child to balk, scream, cry, or shout, "I hate you" or "You never let me do anything . . . you're so mean," or any number of other invectives to express his displeasure at the power you have to interfere with his desires. Don't let this outburst affect your plan of action. Stick to your guns. If you get involved in your child's emotions, you will surely lose. Allow him to be angry, but don't respond in kind. Instead, try reflecting your child's feelings and what can be done about them: "I know this makes you angry, but I'm going to help you get your shoes on so that we can leave. You can practice getting your shoes on when we come home and have more time. A little more practice and you'll have it." Then step right in and do what you have to do.

THINK ABOUT HOW YOU FEEL WHEN SOMEONE POINTS OUT YOUR LACK OF COMPETENCE IN SOME AREA OF YOUR LIFE

Whether it's your spouse questioning your driving skills or your child curling up her nose when you try a new recipe, criticism hurts. With repeated experiences like that, you may never drive while your spouse is in the car or try new recipes. Similarly, children feel discomfort from having their inadequacies pointed out.

Knowing that these feelings are universal is not meant to imply that children rule. Just try to put yourself in their shoes for a minute. Then, before you address a problem, think about what would make you comfortable in the same situation.

PRACTICE MAKES PERFECT

As your child is ready to tackle new skills, set up practice sessions for learning to accomplish new tasks. Establish, in advance, what can and cannot happen. For example, "You can work at putting on your own clothes until breakfast is ready. Then you'll have to allow Mommy or Daddy to help you finish the job." Then keep your word.

When you have even more time, have a practice run, and try to see things from your child's perspective. Your child wants to put on her own jacket? Show her how to lay it out on a step and back into it. She wants to put on her own shoes? Either buy a pair a bit too big so she can easily slip her feet into them, or show her how to open up the shoe so her foot will slip in. Another option, in the early stages of wearing shoes, is hook-and-loop straps rather than laces. As she gets older and more physically adept, she can advance to shoelace tying.

LET YOUR CHILD WORK THROUGH FRUSTRATION

If you're not in a hurry and you see your child's frustration level increasing to the point of explosion, take a few minutes to observe. Working through and coping with frustration is a skill we all need in order to be competent adults. Interfering doesn't give your child an opportunity to practice this skill. Your intervention should come from a position of caring.

First, give your child the words to use to understand the cause of his frustration and some alternatives to achieve success. "Gosh, you're having a really hard time getting your jacket on, and you seem really angry. Can I help you?'' When you offer assistance, you allow your child to save face. When you try to take over, your child has to prove he doesn't need your help. That causes the situation to escalate out of control. Asking questions like ''May I show you another way to do that?'' or making an empathetic statement such as ''I felt the same way when I tried to water-ski the first time'' helps children overcome their feelings of inadequacy.

BREATHE DEEPLY WHEN YOU'RE ANGRY, UPSET, OR DISTRESSED TO BUY YOURSELF SOME TIME

Too many feelings have been crushed with thoughtless, hurtful words. Even though you can, and should, apologize when you say inappropriate things to your child, you can't ever take the words back. Give yourself a time-out. Walk away. Make sure you're clear on what you want or must have for the comfort of the family. Ask yourself if your demand that your child give up his independence in this circumstance is reasonable and appropriate. If you are merely exerting your power without necessity's requiring it, maybe you should reconsider.

TEACH YOUR CHILD TO COMPROMISE

Children approach the world from a totally self-centered perspective. They see themselves as the center of the universe and can't understand why parents don't want the same things they do. They don't defy you as an act of intended disobedience. They want to do what they want to do when they want to do it with no regard for anybody else's needs or wants. The only way they'll begin to understand that they're just one person in a family with others who have different agendas is if it's demonstrated to them regularly. Eventually, as their maturity increases, they'll be able to have a broader understanding of the operation of the family and be capable of the compromises necessary. This skill takes time, practice, and frustration before the child fully integrates the concept.

ACCEPT YOUR CHILD'S NATURE

There's a school of thought that says the way your little one works through his first stage of independence is how he'll approach it as a teenager. Some children feel the need to practice independence with their fists drawn, ready to battle, while others survive it unscathed. While every parent would love to have the child who sails through the growth process like a swan, those children are a rarity. Instead of wishing for what you don't have, appreciate the vehemence with which your child approaches life with a smile on your face and a song in your heart. . . . Who knows what wonderful possibilities exist for this child.

BIBLIOTHERAPY

Bartholomew the Bossy, by Marjorie Weinman Sharmat
I'll Do It Myself, by Jirina Marton
Just Because I Am, by Lauren M. Payne
Leo the Late Bloomer, by Robert Kraus

LYING

"I'M TELLING THE TRUTH!"

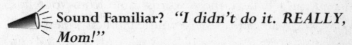 **Sound Familiar?** *"I didn't do it. REALLY, Mom!"*

You decide to take the dog for a walk only to notice a huge bald spot on his back end. Appalled, you cry out, "What happened to Sparky?"

Your son looks at you with wide eyes and says, "I don't know."

Upon further investigation, you find a wad of hair in the trash can inside your son's room along with his kiddy scissors. "Steven," you call suspiciously, "did you cut Sparky's fur?" "No, I didn't do it. Really!" he says, standing firm.

The Tune Your Child Sings: *"If I wish hard enough, it won't be true."*

Young children aren't capable of any sort of real deception. What adults refer to as lies are really the result of "magical thinking." Kids believe: If I wish hard enough that it didn't happen, it didn't, and If I say I didn't do it, I didn't, and If I give the answer Mom and Dad want to hear, they'll quit asking.

Low Notes: *"Remember Pinocchio!"*

Patch of dog hair in hand, you feel you've caught your child in the act. Outraged, you point an accusing finger and say, "You're lying to me. You did it. I'm really angry with you. Now you're in twice as much trouble—for using the scissors on Sparky and for lying about it." Then you pull out all the stops and give him a line your mom used to feed you: "Remember what happened to Pinocchio when he told a lie?"

You can't believe those words came from your lips. Worse yet, you can't believe your child lied—despite all the evidence. You're sure he's on the path to sociopathic behavior and wonder if he'll ever be trustworthy. You worry about what could be so wrong with your parenting technique that you're raising a liar.

▰▰▰ Stop! Rewind Your Own Tape: *The check is in the mail.*

The banker who holds the mortgage called to say he hasn't received this month's payment. Fingers crossed, you say in amazement, "Oh really? I mailed it a week ago." In reality, you're waiting until you get paid tomorrow before you send the check that you've backdated because you're so embarrassed that finances are tight.

Adults lie for many of the same reasons children do. They want to get out of doing something, don't want to disappoint someone, want to avoid trouble, and feel embarrassed by their behavior. Grown-ups also lie to protect someone's feelings—something that kids don't do naturally but something we teach them to do. "No, I don't mind going," you say, and then complain to your family for days. "Sure I'd be happy to volunteer," you say, rolling your eyes at your spouse.

🎵 High Notes: *"Learn to own up to your mistakes."*

When you find the dog hair in your child's trash can and he denies involvement, you look him in the eye and say, "I can see by the hair in the trash can that you cut Sparky's fur. We need to talk about what scissors are used for."

Your child pleads, "But I didn't do it!" You say, "I know it's sometimes hard to tell the truth when you think I'll be angry or disappointed with you. But lying makes the problem worse. You need to learn to be responsible and own up to your mistakes."

"But I didn't do it," he cries.

You begin to question whether your child *is* telling the truth. You can't prove that a friend or cousin didn't perform the act. So instead of focusing on the lie, focus on the deed. "We are not discussing whether you did it or not, we're talking about how you use scissors—and you do not use them or let a friend use them on animals or people. You won't be able to use your scissors for a few days."

Adults often assume children to be much more capable than they really are. They believe children misbehave willfully, with the intent to disobey. However, there is little truth to this. Children behave in context, while parents interpret misbehaviors out of context. Few parents take the time to consider what's going on inside their child's immature-thinking brain.

Lying is related to moral development. Research indicates that until the age of seven, children lack the mental sophistication to deceive with the degree of intensity to cause concern. In other words, their lying is not premeditated or well planned. They just say what they think they should say at the moment. However, that a child doesn't lie well because of a lack of moral development doesn't make lying okay. Children must learn, as soon as possible, about socially acceptable behavior. Lying is not acceptable and when they do lie, they must be confronted with alternative behaviors immediately. It's a parent's job to seize the opportunity to teach their child the difference between reality and wishful thinking. Here's how:

UNDERSTAND WHY KIDS LIE

There are a number of reasons a young child speaks in untruths: She didn't realize what she'd done was wrong, she doesn't want to be punished, or she doesn't want to disappoint those people closest to her, her parents. While you may think, Ah ha, she doesn't want to be punished, therefore she *knows* what she did was wrong and she's protecting herself, in reality, survival is a basic instinct. If children really knew how to lie, they wouldn't be so bad at it.

DON'T SET UP YOUR CHILD BY ASKING QUESTIONS TO WHICH YOU ALREADY KNOW THE ANSWERS

When you catch your child doing something she shouldn't be doing, don't ask the obvious "Did you do that?" As a self-protecting human, a child's instinct is to answer "no" even before she thinks of the consequences of her answer. Instead of asking the obvious, discuss what you observed. "I saw you take Molly's coloring book. You need to give it back to her." If your child says, "I didn't take it," you can respond, "I didn't ask you if you took it, I told you to give it back to her. When someone has something we want, we ask if we can play with it. If the person says no, we don't take it, we wait our turn. Now give it back.''

IS YOUR BEHAVIOR ENCOURAGING YOUR CHILD TO LIE

If we accept that children lie because they don't want their parents to be angry with them, it's important to examine your response to your child's behavior to see if you actually, unwittingly, encourage your child to not tell the truth.

Even if you catch your child red-handed, she doesn't realize you can see her guilt. She just knows that saying, ''No, I didn't do it'' seems to be the right answer based on the anger in your voice when you asked the question. Kids can read our tone of voice and body language. If you stand there with ''that look in your eye,'' your child goes into protectionist mode.

Instead of pointing your finger or angrily accusing when you find your child doing something against your wishes, try another tact. Let's look at an example played out in two different ways. There's Junior, standing with the evidence all around him—cookie crumbs on his face, his shirt, and the floor. In an accusatory tone you ask, ''Did you eat a cookie after I told you not to?'' Frightened by the prospect of the consequence, he shakes his head no.

Actually, asking him if he's disobeyed you is silly. Of course he did, you can see it in his bulging cheeks. The minute you asked the question, you forced him to deny his actions.

Now picture this. You walk in and there's Junior,

chomping away. "Junior," you say, "I told you not to eat those cookies. They were for after dinner; now you won't have any with the rest of us at dessert time. Go to your room until dinner is ready." What you've done here is describe what you saw and the discipline appropriate for not following the rules. You didn't force your child to be on the defensive.

If, however, when you send your son to his room he shouts back in a voice garbled by a mouth filled with cookies, "I didn't eat any," stay calm. Saying, "Now you're lying to me and are really going to get it!" won't teach your child anything, because he doesn't really grasp the concept of lying. Instead, deal with what you know to be true. "I can see by the cookie crumbs spilling off your chin that you ate some cookies, so telling me that you didn't is just not true." (Notice the word *liar* wasn't used.) "When you do something you know you're not supposed to and get caught, I expect you to tell the truth. If you don't, then I'll always have trouble believing you when I ask a question."

AVOID THE "IF YOU TELL ME THE TRUTH, YOU WON'T BE IN AS MUCH TROUBLE" TRAP

When you are confronting a child who *may* have broken a rule, but you don't have absolute proof, avoid the old parental saw "If you tell me the truth you won't be in as much trouble." If your child has done something worthy of discipline, telling her that the truth will erase the deed is counterproductive.

The message should be "If you lie you'll be in greater difficulty." This spells out the consequences from which the child has to choose—yogurt or deep yogurt!

WHEN YOUR CHILD OWNS UP TO HIS BEHAVIOR, EVEN WHEN THERE'S A DISCIPLINARY ACTION FOR THE BEHAVIOR, THANK HIM FOR TELLING THE TRUTH AND REINFORCE ITS IMPORTANCE

The story of "The Little Boy Who Cried Wolf" is an excellent parable to demonstrate the cost of lying.

IF YOU DON'T KNOW FOR CERTAIN THAT YOUR CHILD LIED, GIVE HER THE BENEFIT OF THE DOUBT

There will be situations when you really don't know what happened and can only assume. If you're sure beyond a moral certainty that you know the truth, that's fine for doling out appropriate discipline. But if you're not sure, be very careful. You don't want your child to learn that telling the truth doesn't matter because you're not going to believe her anyway. Instead, if the possibility exists that your child is telling the truth, let her know you accept her response as factual and then move on.

For example, imagine your four-year-old daughter and a friend are playing with wood blocks, some dolls, a toy truck, and unlimited imagination. All of a sudden you hear a crash-bang and go running into where they're playing. The two girls are standing there in wide-eyed surprise and your favorite lamp is in pieces. "What happened?" you shout angrily. "How did you break my lamp?" The girls begin to cry. "We don't know," they exclaim. "We were driving the dolls over the block bridge and under the table when the lamp just fell. We really weren't doing anything, honest!"

You have no information that tells you otherwise. All you have is a broken lamp and two crying four-year-olds.

It may have been an accident; they bumped into the table with the truck, and the lamp fell. Or they may have been trying to turn the lamp on and knocked it over. You've had previous experiences with your daughter trying to do things beyond her ability, and it wouldn't surprise you one bit if she actually knocked the lamp over. But you don't know the facts, and without them, giving your child the benefit of the doubt is the better choice— even if you're wrong. While you may think you've now supported your child's lying habit, in fact what you've done is send a message of trust. This will go a long way in fostering her moral and ethical development. Living up to your trust is more important than living down to your distrust.

IF THE PREPONDERANCE OF THE EVIDENCE SO CLEARLY POINTS TO A STORY OTHER THAN WHAT YOU ARE BEING TOLD, HOLD YOUR CHILD TO THE FACTS AS YOU SEE THEM

If in the lamp scenario you truly know what happened, you might say, "I can see that you were trying to turn the lamp on even after I told you to ask me to help you do that. I need you to tell me the truth!" With eyes lowered and tears falling, your daughter's next response will be fairly typical for this age. "It was an accident." Children think those magic words will exonerate them from any and every error in judgment.

"I know it was an accident," you say. "You wouldn't have broken the lamp on purpose. You needed to tell me that when I first asked what happened. Now I'm angry because my lamp is broken and because you didn't tell me the truth." Depending upon your personal plan of disciplinary action, you can ask your child what she thinks should happen or you can impose whatever consequence you deem appropriate.

THANK YOUR CHILD FOR AN APOLOGY BUT STILL FOLLOW THROUGH

The second most common refrain after "It was an accident" is "I'm sorry." Kids also think those special words will save them from experiencing the consequences associated with inappropriate behaviors. The belief that remorse, by itself, can wipe clean a slate of misdeeds is being observed on a daily basis in courtrooms across the country. When the day comes for sentencing, defense attorneys are saying, "Go easy on my client, he's really sorry for what he did."

When your child says, "I'm sorry, I didn't mean for that to happen," thank her and let her know you're sure her behavior was not purposeful, but that she went against house rules and must pay the price of a bad choice. To require an action from your child beyond the words helps reinforce the concept of thinking before acting. You might ask your child what she thinks she could do to make up for her bad judgment. "You made your friend cry when you took that toy away; what do you think you could do to make her feel better?"

DON'T FORCE A CHILD TO APOLOGIZE

Requiring a child to say "I'm sorry" will surely backfire with a defiant child who says, "No, I don't want to apologize!" You can't make a child do what she doesn't want to do, and you certainly don't want the battle: "No, I won't apologize." "Yes you will or you'll go to your room!'' What are you going to do if your child chooses to go to her room and doesn't say I'm sorry?

Children have pride but lack the maturity to know how to save face. You may think they're being stubborn, but they don't have the tools for any other response. Putting a child's back against the wall creates a no-win situation for parent and child.

But if you say, ''When you have done something to make your friend feel better, you can go back to playing,'' you give your child a choice and she'll probably be less adamant in her lack of cooperation. Otherwise, she'll stand with arms folded and say, ''Make me!''

REALIZE THAT YOUNG CHILDREN DON'T INTENTIONALLY HURT PEOPLE

When one toddler hits another, he's not considering his friend's feelings. That other child is merely an obstacle keeping him from what he wants, and he's using the only tools he has to persevere. If you were to ask this child, ''Why did you do that?'' he would not be able to respond. If he said, ''I didn't do anything,'' he'd not be lying. In his mind, he was trying to accomplish a personal goal, and he has no awareness that anything happened. His surprised look in response to your anger is genuine, as if to say, ''What did I do? I just wanted that truck, so I took it!''

HELP YOUR CHILD UNDERSTAND THE CONCEPT OF HURTFUL WORDS—EVEN IF THEY'RE THE ''TRUTH''

A child's thoughts go from idea to mouth without consideration. How do you teach your child not to hurt people's feelings with his words while teaching him about truth telling? Imagine your child sitting on Grandpa's lap and suddenly blurting out, "Grandpa, your breath smells yucky." If you say, "Don't say that, it's rude," your child thinks, But you told me to tell the truth, and his breath smells yucky.

Children need to experience several years of life before they're capable of considering the impact of their words. When your child speaks the truth but his words are painful, take him aside and explain how his words have hurt someone's feelings. Help him understand that he doesn't have to say everything he thinks.

FIND KIND WORDS THAT BALANCE TRUTH AND TACT

Teach your child how to speak the truth without being hurtful. If your child opens up a birthday present she thinks is going to be a new toy only to find out it's a book she already has, without guidance she's going to protest loudly and to all who will listen. She doesn't consider the impact of her words on the gift giver.

One way to minimize this kind of behavior is to hold a practice session before an event where something like this could occur. Suggest to your child the kind of words she can use so she can remain truthful but not hurt somebody's feelings: "Grandma, thank you for the book, I appreciate your giving it to me" or "Grandma, it was very thoughtful of you to bring me a present for my birthday." While this may sound impossible for children to accomplish, they'll try to live up or down to your expectations as long as they know what those expectations are.

IF YOUR CHILD DOES SPEAK INAPPROPRIATELY, REMEMBER THAT YOUR FIRST REACTION IS USUALLY BASED ON YOUR OWN EMBARRASSMENT

Yelling at your child for speaking an unsuitable truth raises more questions for her than it does answers. Respect your child by taking her aside and explaining that her words were hurtful. Discuss it in terms of how she would feel if someone said those same words to her. Children are capable of learning life's lessons if parents take the time to teach them.

It will still be several years before a child has organized the information that leads to a healthy understanding of which comments are acceptable and which are not. Why is telling Uncle Bob that his mustache is nice okay, but saying the same thing to Aunt Lydia isn't all right? How come you can tell Daddy that you like his hair but you can't tell Granddad how shiny his bald head is? Children do not differentiate these observations for quite some time. They speak from the heart: What I see is what I will talk about!

WATCH YOUR LITTLE WHITE LIES

A recent research project demonstrated that adults lie on the average of twenty-seven times a day . . . mostly those pesky "white lies" that are said to avoid hurting someone's feelings. Though you may think white lies are harmless, children listen and learn from their parents. If you say to your child, "If that's Aunt Bobbi on the phone, tell her I'm not here," your child will not understand why it's okay for you to lie, but not him. Instead, demonstrate truth telling: "If that's Aunt Bobbi, tell her

I'll call her back later." There's no need for explanations, but there is a need to be truthful. Anything less, and your child will learn behaviors you don't like, at the feet of the master—YOU!

REINFORCE MORAL AND ETHICAL BEHAVIOR

With practice and maturity, children will develop a strong sense of right and wrong. When they say or do the right thing, make sure you comment positively. That way, you'll reinforce appropriate behaviors you appreciate and send messages that will guide your child down the right path.

BIBLIOTHERAPY

A Big Fat Enormous Lie, by Marjorie Weinman Sharmat
The Adventures of Pinocchio, by Collodi (Carlo Lorenzini)
Ernie's Little Lie, by Dan Elliott
The True Francine, by Marc Brown

MANNERS

"PLEASE AND THANK YOU."

Sound Familiar? *"Say thank you, Johnny."*
It's your child's fifth birthday and he's opening Grandma's present in front of an audience of relatives. Instead of saying thank you for the toy truck your mother so carefully chose, your son protests, "But I wanted a race car!"

Mortified, you coax your child to apologize and tell Grandma "thank you," but the damage has already been done. You're embarrassed, your mother feels bad, other relatives think your son's an ingrate, and now your child is in a heap of trouble.

The Tune Your Child Sings: *"But I don't like that present. Do you want me to lie?"*
During the preschool years, social rules are beyond a child's comprehension. They see themselves as the center of everyone else's universe. Kids believe they deserve what they want, without having to use the "magic words" of please and thank you. And because they've been told time and again to tell the truth, they don't understand the difference between being polite and lying. If your son doesn't want that toy, shouldn't he say so?

Low Notes: *If you could beam yourself up, you would.*
You tell your son how rude he's been and try to get him to make Grandma feel better. "Say you're sorry," you

coach. Then, so that the others know you're interested in your child's good manners, you state, "And if you don't like the truck, there's plenty of other boys and girls without toys who would."

You go through the birthday party motions, but in truth you can't wait until your guests leave and you get your child alone to teach him some manners.

Stop! Rewind Your Own Tape: *Open mouth, insert foot.*

You wake up on a Saturday morning craving waffles, and then discover there is no syrup. Disappointed, you take a shower instead. When you return to the kitchen, you realize your husband has dashed to the store and bought you the rich maple syrup you love. But instead of just thanking him, you ask if he remembered that you also needed milk and shampoo. As the words come out, you wish you could pull them back, but it's too late. His feelings are hurt. What could have been a wonderfully special moment is lost forever.

How many times have you said something you shouldn't have? As an adult, you know better, and you beat yourself up every time you speak before you think. A child who's just started learning social graces doesn't have the conscience or the sensitivity to discern when his words will have hurt someone. It's our job as parents to teach children good manners, tell them how to deal gracefully with disappointment, and set the example for polite behavior and respect for others' feelings.

♪ === **High Notes:** *"You hurt her feelings. What can you do to make her feel better?"*

The minute your son blurts his disappointment, you ask to speak with him in private. Your tendency is to make him apologize right at that moment, but you know that his parroting your words won't make things better. Grandma will know your son is repeating the words without any thought, and your son won't learn anything except that Mom or Dad will tell him when to apologize and that words alone will wash away his sin.

Alone with your child in his room, you explain to him how his words hurt Grandma's feelings. You let him know that even though he didn't get the race car, Grandma went to a lot of trouble to pick out the toy truck. You suggest to him that he appreciate the gift because of the effort Grandma made to go to the store, pick it out, buy it, and wrap it so beautifully. You explain that he won't always get what he wants and that he should be happy with what he receives.

"Your words hurt Grandma's feelings, and you need to do something to make her feel better," you say, allowing your child to decide what he needs to do. Amazingly, parents who have high expectations of their child to do the right thing at such moments are often not disappointed.

Though you want your child to understand how grateful he should be, avoid comparing what he has to what less fortunate children don't have. Think about it. When you were little did hearing about the starving children in China ever do anything to make you want to finish the food on your plate? Deal only with your child and avoid comparisons to siblings, friends, or kids in faraway lands.

• • •

Children don't enter the world prewired for social graces. They start out as babies who expect their needs to be met on demand, and they usually are. What starts as a matter of survival develops into learned behavior. You now have a child who has every reason to believe that the world revolves around him, and, being the good parent you are, you reinforce that perception.

Now your child is a little older. Your expectations have changed to accommodate a new belief that an older child is a more courteous child. Your youngster, however, now has to learn a new set of behaviors related to the fact that there are other people in the world with needs and wants different from his. He has to learn to wait his turn, to share, and to say please, thank you, and I'm sorry. These are not automatic behaviors and are often the bane of parents' existence.

How do you turn a self-centered, ME, ME, ME baby into a kind and polite child? Roll up your sleeves and get ready to mentor and manage your child.

CHILDREN REPEAT BEHAVIOR TO WHICH THEY ARE EXPOSED

Research has determined that from birth, babies organize their world into little, manageable compartments of understanding. They store all of the information they're exposed to (bombarded with) and continually work at adapting to and accommodating it. Long before babies are verbal, they've been exposed to a ton of information that they've organized and categorized into useful schemes.

With that in mind, it's even more imperative that parents demonstrate good manners and treat others in a fair, kind way. "Please" and "thank you" are more readily absorbed into the mental structure of the world if children hear them in context, as a matter of routine. *Telling* a child to say thank you is less meaningful than *thanking* a child for doing what was asked.

Children want to be little adults. That's why early stages of dress-up involve playing mommies and daddies. Observing your child during this play will give you real insight into how she's interpreting the lessons you're teaching. Children will repeat the behaviors to which they're exposed. So, if *please*s and *thank you*s are to be normal and natural, they must be peppered into as many interactions with children as possible. Talk about an open window of opportunity!

LIVE AN ETHICAL AND MORAL LIFE

Parents not only have to demonstrate good manners to their children, they must live an ethical and moral life. Don't fall into the "Do as I say, not as I do" routine. Parents who give lip service to "clean" living will have children who try to figure out the best angle to get what they want. If parents take the moral high road, chances are their children will too.

DON'T RELY ON SUBTLE CUES TO TEACH YOUR CHILD THE RIGHT WAY TO DO THINGS

Recognizing that children interpret the world from two feet off the floor allows parents to accept that children will not always respond correctly or understand a lesson being taught in subtle undertones. If you assume that messages are being relayed, you may be disappointed when you find out your child has not mastered a new concept as quickly as would please you.

Each day, we bombard our child with new information that she's expected to absorb, comprehend, and immediately utilize correctly. Think about what it would be like to study a foreign language through a total-immersion program. While you're being barraged with vocabulary, grammar, idioms, and colloquialisms, you can only understand so much. The rest simply won't get absorbed. It will take repeated exposures before you begin to demonstrate your proficiency. It's not for lack of trying that you're not successful; it's more a case of being overwhelmed by all the information. Slowly you'll become more competent, and one day you will look back on the initial foray and laugh at your mistakes. Children need the same understanding and patience that you would afford yourself.

SET UP PRACTICE SESSIONS TO EMPOWER CHILDREN TO BE SUCCESSFUL

When children face situations where new skills are necessary, don't expect them to know what to do automatically. Take the opportunity to show them the manners they'll be expected to display through a dress rehearsal. Have a pretend Thanksgiving dinner to practice table manners; make believe you're in a house of worship to demonstrate how to sit quietly; throw an imaginary birthday party to teach how to greet guests and open gifts graciously. Giving your child an opportunity to practice her manners in a safe place increases the probability that she'll make you proud during the real thing.

POINT OUT EXAMPLES OF GOOD AND BAD MANNERS

Another means of teaching children what constitutes good manners is to show them examples of acceptable and unacceptable behaviors in the community: "Did you hear how that child spoke to his mother? Do you think she liked it when he said that? What else could he have said?" or "Wow, did you see what happened when she remembered her good manners? She was allowed to stand in front of the crowd during the parade. That's what happens when children behave like ladies and gentlemen."

If you expect your child to be successful and teach him to develop the necessary skills, chances are you'll have a well-behaved child. But if you expect your child to embarrass you, he'll sense your frustration and lack of confidence and probably will. Children have an amazing radar system and will deliver exactly what you expect.

POINT OUT ERRORS IN A RESPECTFUL WAY

The social faux pas children make stem from a lack of understanding, not a conscious desire to mess up. Laughing at children when they err, or worse yet, growing angry, becomes an inhibitor for improvement. Accept mistakes as part of the learning process.

If you feel it's necessary to point out your child's errors, show him the same respect you would expect. Take him aside and speak quietly and privately. "Sammy didn't like it when you took the cape away from him. What would have been a better way to get it?" And then guide your child to saying, "I could have asked him if I could have it when he was finished."

"That would have been a good choice," you might say. "Do you want to go try it? Remember, good friends say I'm sorry, too." Wrapped up in that one conversation is a model for appropriate behavior and a direct lesson in social skills. Routine exposure to this kind of dynamic leads a child to successful relationships and personal satisfaction. Ultimately, isn't that one of your goals for your child?

REINFORCE THE MANNERS YOU WANT

When your child demonstrates appropriate social skills, reward her with positive comments. "Thank you for remembering your good manners and using 'please' when you asked for more milk. It shows what a big girl you're becoming." Parents don't realize how powerful these kinds of statements are in encouraging and supporting behaviors that are highly valued in our society.

DON'T COMPARE SIBLINGS' MANNERS

Parents with more than one child will often use the "good" sibling as a model for the child who is struggling with manners. (Refer to the "Sibling Rivalry" chapter for more detail on this very sensitive subject.) Rather than engendering change in the "difficult" child, such comparisons cause conflicts that can last a lifetime. "Why can't you be more like your sister" is a plea that at its core is an unreasonable expectation. To encourage sameness between children denies uniqueness. The more spirited child will go out of her way to be different and more troublesome. Children often don't learn their lessons from observing other children in the real world. The behaviors they want to emulate in early childhood are those of their parents and other important adults in their lives.

BE PATIENT

Good manners will happen, eventually. It will take the expansion of language skills and experiences. It will require growing out of the egocentric stage into a broader relationship with the rest of the world. It will take making mistakes, practicing, and making more mistakes until children finally get it right.

Children who observe the important people in their lives using appropriate social behaviors and who receive positive rewards for behaving in socially acceptable ways will adapt these behaviors into their world scheme. After a while, your child won't have to think about right and wrong; it will come as naturally as night following day.

BIBLIOTHERAPY

Dinner at Alberta's, by Russell Hoban
Manners, by Aliki
Richard Scarry's Please and Thank You Book, by Richard Scarry
What Do You Say, Dear?, by Joslin Sesyle
Perfect Pigs: An Introduction to Manners, by Stephen Krensky

SHOPPING

"CAN I GET A COOKIE, ICE CREAM, CAR, DOLL . . . ?"

Sound Familiar? *"I want! I want! I want!"* You're down to your last bagel and you can't put it off any longer. You grab your three-year-old to go to the grocery store, teeth already clenched at what the excursion will undoubtedly bring. Within two minutes, she is upset because you won't buy the chocolate layer cake in the bakery case and is pleading to hold the lobsters at the seafood counter. All you want is enough groceries to get you through dinner and breakfast, but you can't concentrate because you're daydreaming about what it was like to be single, when a shopping trip was relaxing and fun.

The Tune Your Child Sings: *"She's buying things for her. I want something, too."* Grocery stores are like Disneyland to kids. The sounds, smells, and colors overwhelm their senses. They want everything they see—especially the sugarcoated cereal, candy, and toys advertised on Saturday-morning cartoons. It's theirs for the asking—or so they think. With Mom or Dad engrossed in reading shopping lists and labels and gazing up and down shelves to find products, a kid easily gets ignored in a grocery store. It takes all she can muster to get even a nod of attention.

Low Notes: *"Get me out of here!"*

The loving mom you long to be quickly metamorphoses to the madwoman you hate. You buy what you can and grab your daughter to check out. You're so angry, you lecture your darling all the way home and then send her to her room. When all is said and done, you despise grocery shopping, your child, and more than anything else, yourself.

Stop! Rewind Your Own Tape: *Tool shopping is boring.*

As a woman, have you ever been sentenced to the tool department with your "Tool Time" husband? He's totally engrossed and enthralled by all the gadgets, but to you one wrench looks like another. You just wish you could escape to Victoria's Secret. Well, that's how your children feel. That's why they sneak off to the toy aisle while you comparison-shop for the breakfast cereal.

High Notes: *Planning ahead saves sanity.*

As much as you can, try to plan your grocery shopping trips for when neither you nor your child is tired or hungry. Before you leave for the store, tell your youngster what you are going to buy and let him know there will be a treat if his behavior warrants it. When you arrive at the store, remind him of your expectations. "Remember, if I keep hearing, 'Buy me this and I want that,' you will get nothing." Then, during the shopping trip, try to involve your little one as much as possible so he doesn't get bored. That may mean asking a two-year-old to hold the list or look for the products on the shelf. A four-year-old can take items off the shelf and put them into the cart. And as any mom who has stepped inside a store with preschoolers knows, helping Mom won't last for long. So bring a snack, book, or handheld game to occupy your child.

Shopping is one of those things we do with kids that can easily suffer from what's called "negative synchrony." It works like this: If every time you think about taking your child grocery shopping you imagine how terrible it will be and become angry, you create an attitude that expects bad behavior. In that pattern, even the slightest irritation grows into a mega annoyance. Your child has no chance to succeed and lives down to your expectations.

When you are in one of those "moods," the wisest thing may be to postpone your shopping trip. If you must go, write not only your grocery list but a list of all your child's good characteristics. That will help refocus your thinking. You'll realize that your child really isn't that bad; you just see him in a negative light when you are tired or frustrated.

Here are concrete tips to make shopping more pleasant for you and your kids.

KNOW YOUR CHILD'S TIME LIMITS

Children do not set out to make a trip to the store a battleground of wills (and won'ts). Any kind of shopping excursion is an exercise in restraint for a child who is short on patience and long on attention-getting techniques. The length of your shopping trip should depend on the age and maturity of your child.

Children between the ages of two and three reach their boredom limit within minutes. It doesn't matter if you're shopping for groceries, kids' clothes, or toys. Toddlers lack the mental maturity to sustain the interest and energy necessary to behave well during a trip to the store that lasts longer than ten to fifteen minutes.

Children between four and six will exhibit some patience when taken on a shopping outing, but this will abate quickly if they feel you're more interested in shopping than you are in them.

PLAN AHEAD FOR SHOPPING EXCURSIONS

If you are going to the supermarket, make a list of what you need. This will help you get in and out of the store before little tempers flare. Most grocery stores' customer service departments have aisle charts of where various items are located. Learn your store's footprint so that you can write your list in the order in which you will find the items in the store. That way, you won't have to keep wandering back and forth.

When you're reading the newspaper's food section or leafing through a magazine, cut out pictures of items you normally buy. Put them in a plastic bag or coupon pouch and take them with you when you shop. Then, as you look for items on your list, show your child the products you want him to help you find. You can also save a few empty containers and take them with you to the store so your child can find new ones that match.

PREPARE KIDS FOR THE TRIP

A little bit of effort on your part *before* the shopping adventure will increase the pleasure factor. Let your child know the reason why you are going shopping. Tell him what you plan to buy and how long it will take.

Before you leave for the store, remind your child of your expectations. He wants to please you, but he doesn't always know what will earn your praise, so tell him. Be specific about the type of behavior you desire and the positive and negative consequences if he does or doesn't do as you instruct. Rather than telling him to "be good," use concrete examples: "I will really be proud of you if we can get our shopping done without my having to remind you not to touch things we are not going to buy" or "Remember, Mommy will decide what we are buying, so if I say no, please don't keep asking me. If you whine or cry or throw something, the shopping trip won't be any fun. However, if you help Mommy shop with a happy face, you will be able to . . ." Fill in the blank: pick out a small treat at the store, have time to stop by the food court for a cold drink, or whatever works for your child and you. Describing the positive consequence of desired behavior gives him something to work toward.

The treat you promise doesn't have to be food (cookies, candy, ice cream, etc.) and does not have to cost money. The reward might be that you will have time to look at the lobsters in the tank by the seafood case (always a favorite), that you will take a few minutes to visit the pet store before you go home, or that you can enjoy a few minutes on the swing before dinner.

INCLUDE YOUR CHILD IN THE SHOPPING DETAILS SO SHE DOESN'T FEEL IGNORED

Give kids attention before they ask for it. Use the shopping trip to teach colors and textures. Show your child how to pick out fruit and vegetables—allow her to try to find ones without bruises and show her how to tell when produce is ripe. Use this time to begin lessons about which foods are healthy and which aren't by talking about what a particular food does for the body or by reading labels and talking about ingredients.

You can also captivate a child—at least for a short while—by talking about how the food is made. Many children think that fruits and vegetables come from grocery stores rather than from trees or gardens.

Along with asking a kid to search the shelves for certain items that look like the ad or the container you brought, send her down the aisle on color or shape hunts. (But let her know the rule is she can't leave the aisle you are in.) Tell your child how many items you are going to buy. Bring flash cards with consecutive numbers and have your child tape a number on each item so they can track how many items have been purchased.

Take along a calculator and have a kindergartner who knows her numbers punch in the price of the items you purchased. Tell your child how much you want to spend. Ask her to track how much you are spending and to warn you if you are going to exceed the preset amount. You can play the same type of game by bringing along paper money. Every time you put an item into the cart, ask your children to give you the price of the product in fake dollars and coins.

Even a child who is too young to help you shop will be less inclined to become restless if she hears you talk and involve her in the shopping. Though doing activities with your child while you shop will increase the amount of time it takes you to finish, a little extra time is worth the pleasant experience you will have with your child.

Shopping can be a wonderful opportunity for instilling family values and teaching kids the value of money. If, however, you are planning a *major* shopping trip, evaluate whether or not you should bring your child.

KNOW WHEN TO BAIL OUT AND GO HOME

Even with the best bag of tricks, adults can't always get kids to cooperate. When all ideas have been tried and have failed, it's time to make some hard decisions. Ask yourself why your child might be acting out. Is he tired or hungry? Could you improve the situation with a piece of fruit or some crackers and juice? Does your child need to be held and comforted? Remember, yelling and demanding obedience will only lead to more tears and frustration (on both your parts).

When you've tried every pacifier you know and your child has just plain reached her maximum level of cooperation or has hit the wall energy-wise, realize it's time for your escape plan. If your young one is acting out uncontrollably, don't force yourselves to continue. Don't ponder another item. Wheel your basket to the checkout counter, pay, and go home. If the lines are long and your child is screaming, leave your cart to the side of an aisle and take him outside for a breath of fresh air. (Other shoppers will thank you for your courtesy.) This change of environment may be just what you both need to alleviate pent-up stress. Once you've both calmed down, you might be able to go back in and check out. But if you can tell that it will take your child more than a few minutes to regain composure, just leave. If possible, alert the store clerk that you will not be able to complete your shopping and that you've left a full cart.

On the way home, bite your tongue to avoid lecturing your child. Simply leaving the store sends a clear message of your disappointment. You might say, "Shopping didn't work today. Maybe we'll be more successful next time. Then we'll have time to ride the merry-go-round." Every positive comment you say to a child is like rewarding him with a big gold star, and adds to his warm fuzzy bank. But every negative message subtracts ten stars. Be careful not to exaggerate your frustration with statements like "I'm never taking you shopping again." Besides proving you're a liar, responding to a child's misdeed this way can turn into a lifelong albatross that weighs him down and can lead to difficulties later in your relationship. Give your child a chance to prove himself—again and again.

A caveat: Be wary of the child who learns that throwing a tantrum will cause Mom or Dad to leave the store or buy treats to quiet him. Follow through with any consequences you specified when you prepared your child for the trip. Don't give your child the treat or visit to the park or video arcade you promised for good behavior if you were, in fact, unable to successfully complete the shopping trip.

THANK A CHILD WHEN SHE HAS DONE A GOOD JOB

We all like to be rewarded for a job well done. When your child has behaved in a manner that pleases you, tell her how pleased you are. You don't need to gush and go overboard; children have a built-in radar detector for parent exaggerations. A simple "Thank you, I really appreciate when you cooperate and help with the shopping'' goes a long way toward achieving repeat positive behavior. The more time you spend extolling your child's virtues, the less time you will have to spend decrying her weaknesses.

WHEN SHOPPING WITHOUT KIDS IS THE BEST DECISION OF ALL

When you have a lot to buy, when you're already frazzled and not in the mood for whining, or when you're shopping for something time-sensitive—such as a new dress for Saturday's party—do yourself and your kids a favor and don't take them along. Make arrangements that give you the time you need to concentrate on shopping. Go to the store when your child is at nursery school, take two hours of vacation time to escape to the mall alone, shop late at night when your spouse can stay home, or reciprocate with a friend or neighbor (''Can you watch my child for a few hours while I shop, and I'll watch yours when you need to go?''). Taking your child shopping with you and letting her run around because you are too tired to put up with her antics is not only unpleasant for other shoppers but will lead to tears and tantrums—most likely yours!

BIBLIOTHERAPY

What Will We Buy?, by Caroline Arnold
Susie Goes Shopping, by Rose Greydanus
Don't Forget the Bacon!, by Pat Hutchins
Joey on His Own, by Eleanor Schick
The Berenstain Bears Get the Gimmes, by Jan and Stan Berenstain

SIBLING RIVALRY

"I HATE MY BROTHER!"

Sound Familiar? *"I had it first!"*
You and your spouse are sipping coffee in the family room when your moment of silence is interrupted with an all-too-common clash. "I had it first," your six-year-old screams to his three-year-old brother. "Give it back to me or I'm telling Mom and Dad."

"No, mine!" the little one screams.

"I hate you, I wish you were never born," shouts the older sibling just as you get up to head to where they are.

"Mommy! Jeremy hit me!"

The Tune Your Child Sings: *"Mom and Dad will side with me."*
Siblings are rivals. They vie for toys, the right to be first, and their parents' attention. For the most part, this rivalry is healthy. It's how parents deal with it that can turn natural competition into an unhealthy adversarial relationship.

Your children suffer a sense of insecurity with their brothers and sisters. They believe the other child is more powerful, more liked, and more competent. Unconsciously, they want to be the best. And the only way they know to become king of the hill is to physically or verbally push the other one out of the way. If they can't accomplish this goal, they often fight and force their parents to take sides—hopefully theirs.

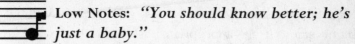 **Low Notes:** *"You should know better; he's just a baby."*

You enter the fray and make an arbitrary decision based on no information other than cries heard from another room. "Jeremy, how many times have I told you not to hit your brother?" you scold your oldest son. "Now go to your room and don't come out until you're ready to apologize."

Stop! Rewind Your Own Tape: *"I'll prove I'm the best."*

Imagine your spouse telling you with real affection that he's bringing home a co-spouse. Over my dead body, you think. I'll show my spouse I'm superior. When the new spouse isn't looking, I'll make her look stupid. Then everyone will know I'm the best!

Sound inane? Well, if that scenario is too far-fetched, just conjure up images of colleagues at work outmaneuvering one another for their boss's attention.

Kids act similarly as they try to find their position within the family. It's natural to want to be the favorite, and kids will do anything to tip the balance of power in their direction. If one child is constantly deemed the troublemaker, he'll often try to make trouble on purpose since at least that distinction is better than no distinction at all.

High Notes: *Give kids power to solve their own differences.*

Try to stay out of sibling squabbles as much as possible, but when physical violence erupts, get involved without taking sides. If age-appropriate, ask each child what he identifies as the problem and how it can be solved. If the kids give you the typical "I don't know," offer possible win/win choices. "I see you're fighting over the truck. Could you get another truck to play with? Could one of you find something else to do? Or could one of you play with it for a few minutes and then give the other a turn?"

Listen to your children's reactions to your suggestions. If they can't agree on a compromise and discipline is necessary, dole it out equally. If you send one child to his room, you send the other to his room as well. If one child loses his privilege to play with the toy, so does his sibling.

Remember, you weren't there and you don't really know what happened or who instigated the squabble. A natural reaction is to take sides—especially that of the younger or less-aggressive sibling. Don't let prejudice sway justice.

How parents respond to sibling rivalry dictates how destructive the competition will become. Always siding with one child over the other or making routine comparisons to get one child to change his behavior are tactics that will probably backfire. Try to stay out of your kids' rivalry problems and give them the chance to solve them on their own.

DON'T COMPARE YOUR KIDS TO ONE ANOTHER

Remember, each child has different strengths and weaknesses, and it's unfair to compare. Even though they have the same parents, siblings may be no more the same than if you went to the local mall and chose two children from among the hundreds running around. Siblings aren't identical to each other—they're unique individuals. Expecting kids to perform at the same level is unfair and dangerous.

DON'T THINK YOU HAVE TO LOVE ALL YOUR CHILDREN IN THE SAME WAY

Love each child for himself or herself. That alone will go a long way toward supporting positive sibling relationships.

FORGET THE FANTASY OF TWO PEAS IN A POD

When parents are expecting their second (or subsequent) child, they imagine their kids being best friends always, never fighting, and always supporting one another. While that sounds ideal, it's as far from reality as you can get. Siblings can be best friends in the long run, but there will be many times in the short term when they'll be as estranged as Cain and Abel.

RECOGNIZE THAT WHAT YOUR KIDS ARE REALLY DOING IS COMPETING FOR YOUR ATTENTION, AFFECTION, AND SUPPORT

When there is more than one child, parental "gifts" must be divided, and one child will always feel that someone is getting more than she is. This is just a natural component of family relationships.

UNDERSTAND BIRTH-ORDER DYNAMICS

When it comes to siblings, the older child will *always* be older and the younger child will *always* be younger! And along with birth order come some inalienable rights. The older child will attain skills, responsibilities, and perks that the younger child will be denied until she is older. The younger child will always be the baby, often expected to do less, seen as more vulnerable, and always riding on the coattails of an older brother or sister whose sweat and toil eased the way. The concept of an unaltering birth order is way beyond your children's understanding. When they see their older or younger sibling getting something they don't have, the battle cry "That's not fair" reverberates throughout the house. You're the one who has to be empathetic without enabling unhealthy behavior.

In most cases, younger children look up to older siblings as mentors and role models. They want to be just like them. Older children look down upon these adoring annoyances and wield their power as swords. What's a child to do?

Easy. He can enlist Mom and Dad in his effort to engage his older sibling. Or, if he is feeling slighted, absolutely certain that Big Sister is getting more from Dad than he is, he might be inclined to attempt to get Sister in trouble so Dad would rather be with him than with her. Children learn quickly what works. If you buy into it, they have total control and you have none!

AVOID FEEDING YOUR CHILDREN'S INSECURITY REGARDING THEIR SIBLINGS

We all have some degree of insecurity when it comes to siblings. Parents, unwittingly, feed this with statements like "How come I don't have to do that for your sister?" or worse yet, "Why can't you be more like your brother? He never gave me any trouble."

Children are unique individuals with *shared* character-istics, not identical ones. Your children are each a com-bination of genetic information from both Mom and Dad and thousands of years of evolution. If conception took place one second sooner or one second later, your children would be entirely different. They'd have dif-ferent personalities, temperaments, physical characteris-tics, and developmental timetables. It doesn't mean one child is better than the other, only that each child is different, and that difference must be nurtured, not squashed.

When you attempt to deny your child the right to develop to her full potential because she's so contrary to what you expected or so unlike your other children, you do nobody any favors. When you send subtle messages to children that say "I value certain characteristics pos-sessed by your sibling," the other child feels bad. "You're the pretty one" and "You're the smart one" messages cause the pretty one to feel stupid and the smart one to feel ugly. Each child will believe that the characteristic of the other is the one you prefer. Children need to be celebrated for their uniqueness.

BE CONSCIOUSLY AWARE OF HOW YOU TREAT EACH CHILD

Does your child have a legitimate complaint about favor-itism? Do you spend more time with one sibling than you do with the other? Do you blame one child more than her brother or sister? Be honest with yourself, even if it means keeping a secret scorecard to evaluate your actions or asking a spouse or friend to help you expose the truth.

TRY TO GIVE EACH CHILD SOME INDIVIDUAL TIME

Even if it's only a few minutes a day, children cherish undivided attention. And if they're given it freely, they won't have to fight for it. Take turns playing one on one with each of your children, or set time aside to read to one all by herself. When the younger child goes to sleep, spare a few minutes for the older one. When the older one is occupied or at preschool, focus on the younger one. When your children get a little older, you may even want to make a date to go out for pizza or a romp in the park with just one of your children, switching off so that each gets a turn to be in the spotlight.

DON'T ASSUME ONE SIBLING IS TO BLAME MORE THAN THE OTHER

If you do, you'll confirm each child's feelings of insecurity and jealousy. The older or more aggressive child will think, See, Mom and Dad really don't love me. The younger child will think, Wow! I'm really powerful; I just have to scream and Mom comes to my rescue. And even though on the outside that child may seem to like the way such power feels, having *all* the power can scare kids. They want their parents to be in charge. When adults abdicate their role, kids wonder if their parents really can take care of them. In addition, kids have an innate sense of fairness and they know if they've been rewarded undeservedly, which again can make Mom and Dad appear out of control.

ACT AS MEDIATOR, NOT REFEREE

Try to teach your children how to solve their own problems; it's a necessary skill for survival and successful adulthood. After all, as they get older you won't always be there to protect and defend them. Rather than take sides, (if the children are verbal) ask each to give his version of the truth. Don't make any judgments about what they tell you, just listen. When each has had a turn, ask them how they think the problem can be fixed. If they can't come up with any ideas, offer a few, including sending them both to their rooms or taking away whatever they're fighting about so neither can have it.

Tell your kids that excuses like "That's not fair, she started it" don't hold water with you. What you want is harmony. You're not a referee. When you haven't seen what happened, you will have to hold them both responsible. When they see you don't take sides, your children will be more than happy to keep you out of their squabbles.

SET HOUSE RULES ABOUT RESPECTING ONE ANOTHER

Children should not be allowed to hurt each other physically or emotionally. When one child starts to call another names, stop it immediately: "I know you're angry, but calling your brother names is not okay. Use other words to tell him why you're angry." When house rules requiring respectful behavior between family members are enforced, children learn appropriate social conduct in a safe place. These rules must be observed by *all* members of the family. If Mom and Dad say nasty things to each other, children won't understand why they have a different set of rules, and therefore won't adhere to them.

UNDERSTAND THAT FAMILY EXPERIENCES TEACH CHILDREN HOW TO OPERATE IN THE REAL WORLD

Brothers and sisters learn how to fight, compromise, and join forces for a common goal. They learn to be responsible for and protect each other. Watch closely. Just when you think that your children will never get along, you'll find them snuggled up in the same bed on a rainy night or one sneaking the other cookies after he's lost the privilege of having dessert.

DON'T FORCE CHILDREN TO LIKE AND PLAY WITH EACH OTHER

The more you force, the more they'll pull apart. Children need alone time, and that has to be respected.

LOVE YOUR CHILDREN FOR WHO THEY ARE, NOT WHO YOU'D LIKE THEM TO BE

Respect and encourage your children's differences. When your child says, "You love him more than you love me," respond by addressing the things that you love about her. Children aren't in competition.

WHAT TO DO WHEN A NEW BABY JOINS THE FAMILY

You can minimize an older child's feelings of rivalry and insecurity when a new baby comes on board by following these steps.

DON'T KEEP YOUR PREGNANCY A SECRET

As soon as you start telling people about your impending new arrival, tell your child. You may think you can keep it concealed, but between your changing body and discussions with friends and relatives, your child will know something is going on. Without facts, she'll make up her own scenario. And remember, children have incredible imaginations. If you don't know how to raise the subject, try reading *How Babies Are Made* by Andrew C. Andry and Steven Schepp to your child. Continually reinforce that the *family*—not just Mom and Dad—is going to have a new baby.

IF THERE WILL BE CHANGES THAT WILL AFFECT THE OLDER CHILD, ARRANGE FOR THEM TO OCCUR BEFORE THE BABY COMES

If your older child is going to start child care, try to have her begin at least a month ahead of the baby's arrival so she doesn't think you're sending her away now that you have a new baby to play with. If your child is moving on to a regular bed and the new baby will get the crib, don't just take it away from the older child. Instead, ask your child for her help, and chances are she'll happily give it. (If you demand obedience, she'll most likely fight with you.) You might say, "Gee, when our baby comes he or she will need someplace to sleep. What do you think we should do?" If your child doesn't readily offer her crib, suggest it gently: "Hey, I have a great idea. What if we give the baby your crib and get you a new bed? Do you think we could do that?" A newborn doesn't need a crib for several months, so weaning an older child from a crib to a bed can occur as slowly as necessary.

If you want to share your first child's clothes with the new baby, try saying, "Our baby is going to need some clothes to wear when he or she's born. Do you have some clothes you might be willing to share?'' When the child feels like a partner in this new ''baby thing,'' she will be less inclined to see the newcomer as an adversary for her parents' affection.

SHOW YOUR CHILD PHOTOS OF WHEN SHE WAS A BABY SO SHE CAN SEE ALL THE ATTENTION YOU SHOWERED ON HER

Discuss the fact that the new baby will need to be fed, diapered, and held, just as she was. Let your child know how lucky the new baby is to have an older sister to help and how important she will be in the growing family.

ENROLL YOUR CHILD IN A SIBLINGS' CLASS

If your child is old enough (check with your local hospital for age limits, usually age three or four), enroll her in a class to prepare her for being an older sister. Using their own dolls, children explore their feelings and learn how to bathe, feed, and hold a baby.

MAKE SURE YOUR CHILD UNDERSTANDS THAT MOMMY IS GOING TO THE HOSPITAL AND COMING HOME WITH A BABY

Hospitals usually instill fear, so a child needs to know that wonderful things can happen in a hospital, too. Prepare your child for the event. Let her know who will care for her until Mom comes home. (Being self-centered, a child's fears will surround who will care for her.)

If at all possible, avoid surprises. Mom shouldn't be whisked off at night, leaving the child to wake up in the morning to find a grandmother, aunt, or friend in her home taking care of her.

TRY TO MAKE YOUR OLDER CHILD FEEL INCLUDED WHEN FRIENDS AND RELATIVES COME TO SEE THE NEW BABY

Be aware that your child may feel left out when others make a fuss over the infant. If your child is old enough, talk about how she might feel: "It will seem strange when everybody comes over and goes right over to the new baby. It might make you angry, and that's all right. Just come and tell me how you're feeling."

It's hard for your child to give up being the center of attention. Getting angry when your child expresses her feelings won't endear the new baby to her.

WHEN TIME ALLOWS, MAKE SURE YOUR CHILD GETS SOME UNDIVIDED ATTENTION

Hiring a baby-sitter so Mom, Dad, and the older child can have a night out tells the child that she is still important. Include the older child in activities involving the baby so she sees herself as part of the circle, not excluded from it.

DON'T EXPECT THE WORST

Children will surprise you. Some older siblings are thrilled by having a new playmate and can't wait until the baby is old enough to be an active participant in family life. On the other hand, when a child understands what having a new baby means, he may also consider the situation from a different perspective: Why do we need another kid, what's wrong with just me? Don't you love me anymore? These are real fears and should not be shrugged off as ridiculous. Instead, if your child appears to be concerned, confront him head-on by reinforcing your love for him and discussing the joys of siblinghood. Point out your own family relationships, talking about your brothers and sisters and how much fun you had and continue to have.

EXPECT OLDER SIBLINGS TO HELP WITH YOUNGER ONES

Having chores to do to keep the house in order is part of being a member of the family. Remember, however, to keep your requests for help age-appropriate. If you make an older child feel as if she's personally responsible for her baby sibling, you could be creating a feeling of resentment that will never go away.

DON'T TELL AN OLDER BROTHER OR SISTER THAT HE/SHE MUST NOW BE THE "BIG BOY" OR "BIG GIRL"

If you do, your child might respond with "I don't want to be a big boy, I still want to be your baby." Being a big boy connotes greater responsibility in life. Instead, assure your child he can be the big brother without being a big boy. Children take your words literally, so be careful which ones you use. If, after the baby comes home, your older child wants to be treated like a baby, accommodate her. If she backslides in using the toilet or wanting to be fed, clothed, and held, give in, but let her know you understand why she's acting that way: "You see your new baby getting attention from me when I feed her, so you want the same thing. Well, I want you to know that I love you and when you were a baby I did these same things for you."

HELP CHILDREN TO SEE THE BENEFITS OF BEING EXACTLY WHO THEY ARE, SO THEY'RE LESS LIKELY TO WANT TO IMITATE THE BABY

Point out the benefits of being a little older and the things the baby can't do because he's just a baby: "You can sleep in a regular bed, put on your own shoes, walk, run, and ride a trike. You can play with your blocks and talk on the phone to Grandma. You can get into your own car seat and eat a hamburger at a restaurant. Poor baby, he needs someone to do everything for him. He sleeps all day and doesn't know the joy of Barney and Big Bird. I think being you is probably more fun than being him."

Remember, each child is different and will react differently to the arrival of a new baby. Support your child's individual concerns with love and understanding.

BIBLIOTHERAPY

Harriet & William & the Terrible Creature, by Valerie Scho Carey
Hard to Be Six, by Arnold Adoff
The Grizzly Sisters, by Cathy Bellows
When I Was Little, by Jamie L. Curtis and Laura Cornell
A Place for Ben, by Jeanne Titherington

TV, VIDEO GAMES, AND OTHER PASSIVE BEHAVIORS

"I DON'T WANT TO GO OUTSIDE."

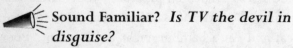 **Sound Familiar?** *Is TV the devil in disguise?*

If you have to listen to *The Lion King* one more time, you swear you'll wrench the video from the VCR and flatten that rotund warthog and laughing hyena. And while you're at it, you visualize taking that video game joystick on a ride to the trash too. You're sick and tired of the power of the tube to keep your child mesmerized when he should be outside running, riding trikes or bikes, and using his imagination.

At least that's how you feel most days. But you've got to admit there are other days—however few and far between—when you actually don't mind the video baby-sitter. At least then your little one is quiet and you don't have to supervise. There are worse things than having your child veg out in front of the television, you console yourself. Deep inside, though, you know that letting television take a major role in your home is detrimental to your family, especially your child.

The Tune Your Child Sings: *"But I don't want to go outside."*

Television, movies, video games, and other passive activities are addictive because they require very little action and virtually no physical energy. It's easy for kids to succumb to passive activities—especially when they're theirs for the asking anytime they want. Besides, it takes too much energy to think of something to do. It's easier to let the television provide the entertainment.

 Low Notes: *"Go out and have fun, right this minute!"*

You snap off the TV and order, "Go outside and play with your friends." Your daughter whines, "But I don't want to. I'm not bothering anybody. Besides, there's no one to play with."

You push your child out the door. She sits on the front steps and mopes, and neither one of you has accomplished anything constructive.

![cassette tape icon] **Stop! Rewind Your Own Tape:** *"I just want to veg out."*

You've just come home from a tiring day at work and have made, served, and cleaned up dinner. You sit on the couch and turn on the television, consumed by this overwhelming desire to do absolutely nothing. Though you know you should go for a walk or ride your exercise bike, you give in to your need to relax and within ten minutes you're fast asleep.

♫ High Notes: *Finding the activity balance.*

You overcome your desire to destroy the videotape and, instead, sit down with your child and discuss the need for physical activity. "After school, you may watch a videotape, play a video game, or play on the computer only for a little while. The rest of the time, you need to be outside playing in the fresh air," you say. "You can make the decision when you want to relax in front of the TV, but it can be for only a half hour a day."

The debate rages on. Is watching television truly harmful to a child's overall growth and development? The answer for the most part is yes. Certainly, in moderation, television and computer games are not going to turn your darling little angel into a vicious mongrel or an unblinking zombie. The problem must be looked at in a larger context.

First, there's a time factor that must be considered. Television watching robs families of time for active togetherness and communication. In many homes, television is the first sound to awaken the family in the morning and the pacifier that lulls it to sleep at night. Conversations are halted with "Ssh, I want to hear that," demonstrating that what is coming from the "tube" is more important than what is happening in your family.

Hours spent watching television is time not spent in pursuit of skill-building activities. Whether those activities promote physical development (e.g., running, bike riding, walking, or just enjoying fresh air) or increase thinking power and expand creativity and imagination (e.g., reading, working on puzzles, or playing with toys), being glued to the television eventually erodes skills and abilities.

Television watching provides an extended circle of friends. But parents have no control over the guests invited into their house for thirty to sixty minutes at a time. Children want to dress, talk, and act like their favorite TV characters. And unfortunately for most parents, we see kids imitating violent, aggressive characters more than loving, thoughtful ones. Television writers and producers develop story lines to sell advertising, not necessarily considering family values of care, respect, and honesty. The influence of television can be seen in the new words, phrases, idioms, and colloquialisms being added to our language. TV's influence is pervasive.

For the naysayers who insist that television doesn't have that much power, consider why cigarette commercials were taken off the air and why advertisers spend billions of dollars on TV commercials. When a celebrity spokesperson spouts the virtue of a product, sales increase dramatically.

The impact of television in our lives cannot be denied. Short of removing the "monster" from your home, what do parents do to help their children find a balance? How do you go against the tide of "Everybody else is watching it, why can't I?" without seeming totally out of touch with reality? Changing your behavior, both in your TV watching and your acceptance of your child's television watching, can have a positive, healthy effect.

To reduce the power television has in your family, try the following.

DEVELOP TV ETIQUETTE AND RULES

Television can be an excellent tool if used with design. It becomes an intruder when it's used indiscriminately. While refraining from using the tube as a baby-sitter may be difficult at first, once you establish new policies and procedures, children can and will adapt to a new routine. But parents *must* be firm and consistent when implementing these changes. If whining and tantrums bring you to your knees, your child will become a robotic slave to the electronic master, and so will you.

LIMIT TV'S AVAILABILITY BY PUTTING KIDS ON A TIME DIET

Determine those times of the day when TV will not intrude on family activities. Don't let it take the place of morning conversation as you start your day together, or evening togetherness as you reconnect at dinner. Allow the TV to be on only during times when it won't interfere with family time. If it's on all the time, it has too much power.

In addition to interrupting family time, overdosing on the boob tube deprives children of physical activity and fresh air, and limits the social development they gain when playing with others. Children will, of course, balk when you limit television watching, telling you there's no one for them to play with and nothing for them to do. This may be true, but should not be the knife to your heart that gets you to back down.

PLAN ACTIVITIES FOR TV "OFF" TIMES

When you first establish blocks of time that the TV will be off, it will seem like there's a "void" in the house, and your child will respond to that vacuum with resistance. Your child won't be accustomed to having to find something to do, because the TV has always provided the entertainment. It's essential, at least in the beginning until your youngster learns how to entertain himself otherwise, that you plan activities to avoid the ''I'm bored'' refrain. Provide materials that will create some excitement. For younger children, that might mean playdough, paints and crayons, glue, paste, stickers, paper, tape, paper punch, rulers, building blocks, dramatic play props, and, of course, books. For slightly older children, all of the above as well as interesting informative materials on photography, gardening, outer space, insects, fish, and the like will fill time.

SACRIFICE YOUR TIME WITH THE TUBE

This new TV diet means Mom and Dad have to give up their willy-nilly TV watching, too. Demonstrate your participation in old hobbies that had been relegated to the back of the closet or the basement in favor of the seduction of TV talk shows or sitcoms. If you go through withdrawal, expect the same from your children.

DEVELOP FAMILY GAMES DURING BREAKFAST AND DINNER THAT ARE AN ENTICEMENT TO STAY AT THE TABLE, RATHER THAN ESCAPE

These games can include making up new words with their own meanings and then using them in sentences. Or each family member can learn about something new and share it with the others. Even young children can participate if the adults support their discoveries with joy and not boredom or impatience.

PLAN FOR TIMES WHEN TV WILL BE A WELCOME VISITOR

When TV *is* allowed, each family member should have some say as to what is watched. Look through a TV schedule at the beginning of the week and create a calendar of approved TV programs. You are the adult and have veto power over shows you consider inappropriate or unacceptable.

Perhaps each family member could get to choose one half-hour program a day, although several family members can pool their time to enjoy a show that lasts an hour or more. On your calendar, write each child's selection in a particular color so he can see the choices at a glance. This helps eliminate the "clicker" battle, because television shows have already been selected. (This probably won't work with adult channel-surfers.)

TV can now be used as a reward for excellence by allowing a child to have extra TV time. It may also add to sibling cooperation and negotiation in making program choices. This method gives parents more power, because they have a better idea of what their kids are watching. And naming shows on a family-"approved" list sends children messages about family values.

DECLARE ONE NIGHT A WEEK TV-FREE/FAMILY NIGHT

If the concept of limiting TV each day seems too radical, another approach is to declare one night a week a TV-free/family-event night. This can be an evening when the family looks through the photo album and you teach your child about her earlier years in the family or of family members long gone or far away. It can be a time when each family member talks about a book he's read or recites a poem she's learned. Use these precious hours for solving puzzles, playing games, or sitting quietly in the same area reading or listening to music. While you may question how these activities differ from watching television, they encourage imagination and raise opportunities for togetherness without having to wait for a commercial to talk.

USE TV SHOWS TO TEACH LIFE LESSONS

On the nights when the tube glows, and if you plan to view only family-acceptable shows, use the programs to teach values. Point out characters who are positive role models versus actors who don't exemplify the standards you want your children to live by.

WATCH OUT FOR THE DOWNSIDE OF COMPUTER GAMES

If the TV time in your house is actually spent playing video or computer games, you have to be concerned about not only messages of violence and aggression but also the lack of interaction with other people and the environment. These are very solitary activities requiring much concentration, limited distractions, and no involvement or participation from others. These games may have some benefit related to problem solving and fine motor coordination, but at what price?

DO YOU KNOW THE CONTENT OF THE GAME CARTRIDGES YOUR CHILD PLAYS WITH

In some cases, computer games are worse than TV because your child is a participant in mayhem and murder. And be careful as your youngster gets older and has access to the Internet. There have been too many cases of kids getting in touch with cyberspace users who have bad intentions.

ARRANGE PLAY DATES TO BRING CHILDREN TOGETHER

If it's tough for your child to find other kids to play with, you may have to make the arrangements. For younger children, these "friends" will most likely be the children of your friends or family members and mates from pre-school/child care. For older children, they may be friends from school, Scouts, sports, or the neighborhood. If these options aren't available, consider enrolling your child in community programs that will bring her into contact with other children her age.

INVEST IN HOBBIES AND GAMES

Without going into hock, try to provide your child with materials and equipment that will be stimulating and enjoyable enough to compensate for the loss of TV and computer games. These might include board games, puzzles, musical instruments, crafts, bug jars, and simple things like clothes for dress-up and buckets and shovels for sandboxes.

PLAY WITH YOUR CHILD

Taking time to play with your child is enjoyable for both you and him. It allows you to return to the joys of childhood. (One of the benefits of having kids is to be able to play with all their neat toys.) Children don't always have to see their parents as "mature, responsible" adults. Flying a kite, roller-skating, or playing a board game together can be therapeutic and enjoyable. It demonstrates to your child that requiring him to do something other than being hypnotized by an electronic medium is not a punishment, but fun. Children need parents to be role models for being joyfully occupied in activities outside of television. Invite your little one to participate in your activities as well—be that baking a cake, making a silk flower arrangement, planting a garden, building a model, or restoring a car.

REAP THE BENEFITS OF TV FREEDOM

Children will adjust to time without television. That doesn't mean there won't still be a fuss when you deny TV watching, but the hassle will diminish as a new family order sets in. There can always be room in the plan for TV specials, family movie rental night, or other occasions that necessitate a change in the normal routine. But in experiments done around the country, when televisions were totally removed from households, after an initial adjustment period most children and families found they gained energy, got more things done, and had a greater investment in the family. And the majority said they wouldn't return to the old days of having the television as a constant companion in their homes.

EVERY MINUTE OF A CHILD'S DAY DOESN'T HAVE TO BE SCHEDULED OR PLANNED

Staring into space has a value. It gives children (and adults) a chance to think! We've become programmed for immediate gratification, no time to waste. But time spent in pursuit of nothing can be time well spent. Thinking is a skill that changes and enhances with brain maturity and brain activity. Practicing thinking, which requires no external physical activity, is hard work that children need to master, just like learning to throw a ball, writing their name, and sitting quietly waiting for their turn.

LET SILENCE BE GOLDEN

Don't let kids learn how to respond to others from watching TV. Television dialogue is scripted, so the actors always have the right thing to say at the right time. Children need to learn to take time to consider the issue at hand and their answer. When silence ensues during a conversation, don't think the moment needs to be rescued with a comment. That only sends the message to children that silences are deadly and discourages reflective contemplation before speaking. Thinking before speaking is a trait most adults are still trying to master.

And at other times, when children are silent and playing alone, don't assume they need to be rescued. Learning to amuse oneself and be alone is another one of those skills that enhance competency and success in adulthood.

BIBLIOTHERAPY

Bored, Nothing to Do, by Peter Spier
Saturday Mornings Last Forever, by Elizabeth Bram
The Berenstain Bears and Too Much TV, by
  Jan and Stan Berenstain
Nothing to Do, by Russell Hoban
The Rainbow Fish, by Marcus Pfister

WHINING AND TANTRUMS

"COME ON, DAD . . . , AH, MOM . . ."

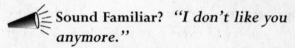 **Sound Familiar?** *"I don't like you anymore."*

You're at the mall with your child and have already bought her the golden palomino horse with Aunt Sally's birthday money. She sees a Barbie in cowgirl clothes and wants it, too. "As soon as you save your money, you can come back and get it," you say reassuringly. But your anxious doll collector doesn't want to wait. "I want the cowgirl Barbie," she whines. "Not now, honey. We've spent all our money. Maybe another day." As you grab her hand to leave, she stiffens her body and won't budge! She pulls away and folds her arms, her lips pouty and her brow frowning. "I want the Barbie! I don't like you anymore."

The Tune Your Child Sings: *"I'll pout until I get what I want."*

If your daughter can't have the Barbie, she can at least get your attention with inappropriate behavior. Young children are naturally egocentric. They need immediate gratification and have no impulse control. Without the maturity to understand delayed gratification, your daughter follows the only course she knows and demonstrates her frustration by looking and acting as angry as she can. She knows the ultimate blow is to tell you she'll like you only if you comply with her wish. If you reward her behavior with attention, she'll learn that whining and tantrums work. And of course, being able to manipulate Mom and Dad is exactly what she wants!

Low Notes: *"I'm bigger; I'll win."*
Angry and embarrassed as others in the store start to stare, you try to exert parental power over your child. "Young lady, you don't talk to me like that. Now come with me right this second or you'll spend the rest of the day in your room!" "No!" she yells back, and starts to cry. You begin to sweat at the pressure, your face flushes, and you suddenly say what you swore you never would. "If you don't stop crying, I'll give you something to cry about!" Clever move. That only makes your child cry louder. You drag her out of the store as other parents thank their lucky stars it's you and not them, and you vow never to take the monster shopping again.

Stop! Rewind Your Own Tape: *Remember the last time you slammed down the phone?* Can you honestly say you've never griped, pouted, or stamped your feet? You've never walked away when someone was talking to you, slammed down the phone in irritation, or cut off a driver who frustrated you? We've all whined, sniveled, growled, and acted irrational when we haven't got our way. Children are no different. It's the way we react to their acting out that determines if their behavior will become a routine form of manipulation.

♫ **High Notes:** *"If you need to cry, I'll be waiting right here."*

The minute your daughter started to whine about the Barbie doll, you could have set her on the right course with the comment "I can't hear you when you whine. When you can talk in a grown-up voice, I'll listen." Then distance yourself from the child so she doesn't get any of the attention she craves. When she realizes her ploy isn't working, chances are she'll tell you she's ready to talk.

If the whining escalates into a tantrum, gather all of your internal resources and don't get angry. Acknowledge that you can understand how she feels—which is 90 percent of what the child wants and needs. You might say, "I know you're angry because you can't have the Barbie now. And if you need to cry, I'll understand. I'll be waiting right over there, so let me know when you're done and we can finish our shopping trip." You have just established that you're the adult in control but you respect your child's feelings. Without receiving the attention they desire, most kids will give in. If your child doesn't stop crying after a few minutes, you need to say, "You know, it looks like you need to cry for a long time, so let's go home" (or let's go get some fresh air). The change of surroundings will often help the child to compose herself.

When the tantrum is over, bring it to a close with words like "Are you feeling better?" or "Are you ready to continue shopping?" Sometimes a simple hug that lets your daughter know you still love her is all she needs. Though your head may be pounding and you feel like curling up and crying yourself, your child needs that reinforcement.

. . .

Children's feelings are just beneath the surface. They lack any sophistication in controlling how they feel or how to express it. They see the world only from one perspective—theirs. This creates a life of perceived unfairness that's the bane of the child's very existence. If you give in to self-centered, attention-getting behavior even once, your child will accept it as a means to an end, and the consequences will cause you to rethink this whole parenting thing. A remote island in the South Pacific will look mighty appealing.

Kids throw tantrums for several reasons. Sometimes it's simply a manipulation to get what they've been denied. Sometimes it's a release of tension, frustration, or fatigue, or a sign your child isn't feeling well. Often, it's a child's way of getting your attention. Younger children use tantrums because they lack the language skills to express themselves and are often deficient in the physical skills that would allow them to be self-reliant. As children pass the age of three to three and a half and four, they become more competent in the world and often exchange whines for tantrums. Both behaviors come from the same source. If your child continues to use these methods as he moves on past the preschool years, observe if there's a pattern to what triggers the outburst or to the end result of the annoying behavior. It's possible that changing the way you deal with these behaviors will have a dramatic effect on eradicating them.

Here are recommendations to help you through humiliating and embarrassing moments that tantrums and whines can create. Handled correctly, some of life's best

lessons can come from a child's most self-centered behavior.

MAKE ROOM FOR ANGER

Some people believe that a child's life is so stress-free
that there should be no room for anger. But anger is a
normal, healthy emotion for persons of every age. Children who are discouraged from or punished for being
angry have no outlet for their feelings. And if left pent
up, this type of feeling can cause physiological damage to
the body. Squelching a child's anger is like baking a
potato in the microwave without first piercing it with a
fork. Without those "outlets," once the potato reaches
a combustible internal temperature, it will explode! As
does the human species.

ACCEPT THAT WHINES AND TANTRUMS ARE
APPROPRIATE (BUT ANNOYING) BEHAVIOR

A tantrum to a child is like a crying jag for an adult.
Sometimes you just have to let it out. You feel better
when it's over. If anybody dared command you to "Stop
that this minute," you'd be insulted, angry, and potentially dangerous to the other person. Tantrums, while
annoying, can be very therapeutic. Rather than approaching the behavior from a position of anger, try to
let your child know that everything is going to be okay.
Anger on your part will most likely escalate the behavior
or cause fear. Neither of these is a desired outcome or
assists a child in learning better ways to handle angry
feelings.

DON'T TAKE YOUR CHILD'S OUTBURSTS OF ANGER PERSONALLY

When your child acts the worst is when you need to love him the most. This means that when a child has a tantrum, parents need to respond in a calm, caring way that says, "Your anger and inappropriate behavior will not make me stop loving you." But love doesn't mean giving in to whines and tantrums. It means setting and sticking to standards and showing empathy as your child tries to comply with the rules. Reacting this way will help your child through the crisis.

USE A TANTRUM CORNER TO CURB HOSTILITY

For some young children, anything that goes against their desire is a crisis. So in addition to calm reassurances, children need to learn new ways to express themselves so they don't have to resort to tantrums. One way to do this is to let your child know the tantrum won't get him what he wants. Create a "tantrum corner" in your house (which could be the child's bedroom, a corner of the kitchen, or anywhere that's away from parental/human interaction). Every time your child uses a tantrum to get your attention or to get something else, direct him to the tantrum corner. Your child should always be allowed (well, almost always) to have his tantrum, but you don't have to be victimized by it. If your child refuses to go, you can either physically assist him, without comment, or you can remove yourself by saying, "I appreciate that you're angry, but I don't want to hear your crying. I'm going in the other room. When you're ready to talk about the problem, I'll be ready to listen." While it's not easy to stay calm in the presence of a screaming child, that demeanor shows you're not affected, and it's key to quelling the obnoxious behavior. It will also give you time to marshal your inner forces to deal with the source of the tantrum, rather than feeling guilty or embarrassed that you flew off the handle.

TRY TO UNDERSTAND THE REASON FOR THE TANTRUM

It often feels like it requires ESP to understand the source of a child's behavior that you find annoying. Remember, a child's behavior is one way she has to communicate. If you can ferret out the reason that a child is behaving poorly, you can help change the behavior. If you try only to stop the behavior without finding its source, you'll experience only a temporary change of behavior.

When your child can't express in words what's wrong, do some soul-searching of your own. Is your child feeling lonely or estranged from the adults in her life? If so, she may lack the necessary skills to reengage in ways that are appropriate, and lashes out by whining, pouting, or throwing a fit. She's not capable of asking for attention, as a spouse who feels isolated does by asking for a hug or kiss as reassurance. Children don't have the ability to say, "I'm feeling apart from you and want you to talk to me." Instead, they fall apart. They hope it will bring you closer and don't yet understand that it will separate you further. Maybe that's why they often behave the best after they've gotten in trouble and you have kissed and made up. Even though it was painful, the two of you reconnected, and feel better for it.

PROVIDE PHYSICAL ASSISTANCE TO CALM A CHILD DOWN

A child's tantrum can easily transcend a simple tantrum and reach out-of-control proportions. When this happens, rather than step *away* from the child, you must step *in* and provide physical assistance to calm him down. Soothing strokes and quiet words will help your little one regain composure. Each child has a different threshold, so a parent must determine for himself when a child's tantrum has crossed over to "out of control."

CREATE A "FEELINGS" BOX

If your child has a low tolerance for not getting her own way, finding a coping mechanism that works for her requires some creative thinking. One idea that has several variations is to create a "feelings" box that includes props for role playing to let your child express her feelings in a safe way. Props can include a puppet, a "magic" wand (any dowel or stick will do), or anything the child can use to help her talk about what made her angry: a noisemaker to help express anger, a mirror so she can practice making angry faces, or some well-chosen pictures of faces that help her identify her feelings. Of course paper, crayons, and markers are always great to help your child draw how she feels. The feelings box doesn't have to be strictly for anger; it can be an outlet for expressing all feelings.

CONTROL ANGER BY SHOWING CHILDREN SAFE WAYS TO EXPRESS IT

It may be that the best treatment for your child's anger is a pops-back-up punching doll or a pillow to hit to allow for a physical release of pent-up feelings that would otherwise lead to a tantrum. Allowing a child to hit something safe *does not* teach a child that hitting is okay! Hitting people is wrong. There are plenty of times in our lives when hitting is part of an activity, e.g., hitting a ball with a bat or hitting a target with a rock, dart, or arrow. When children are shown safe ways to express their feelings, they don't have to resort to behaviors that you find uncomfortable or intolerable. But children will not know what ways are acceptable unless you show them, tell them, and model scenarios to get what you want or to express anger in ways that are socially welcomed.

VIEW WHINING AS ANOTHER PLOY FOR ATTENTION

As with tantrums, paying off whining with your attention only encourages it to continue. However, it's important to consider the source of the whining. Is your child feeling neglected? Is his whining, "Mommy, Mommy, Mommy," just his way of asking to be noticed? Sometimes it's hard to meet the individual needs of each family member when you're striving to meet the needs of the family as a whole. It's easy to overlook a child's need for physical or spiritual attention in the workaday world of providing for his bigger needs of food, shelter, and health.

TURN A DEAF EAR TO WHINING

If whining has become your child's natural way of talking to you, curb the incidence by telling him you can't hear him when he talks like that. If you continually reinforce that you won't respond unless your little one uses a "big boy'' voice, eventually your son will modify his behavior to get your attention.

WATCH THE WAY YOU RESPOND

Parental anger is only a short-term measure in changing a child's behavior. It may help the parent to release tension and frustration, but what does it teach the child? A parent who reacts in kind to a child's temper tantrums, whimpers, and snivels leaves a child confused.

EMPLOY HUMOR TO EASE TENSION

While belittling, embarrassing, or humiliating a child is not worthy of a parent, honest humor can be effective. When your child throws a tantrum worthy of an Oscar, demonstrate her behavior back to her, but in grander fashion. If your child is crying, cry louder in an exaggerated voice. If your child is kicking her feet and banging her fists, do the same in broad farce. Then, while your child is looking at you in stunned amazement, laugh at yourself (not her), pick her up, and give her a hug. This may be the very thing her behavior is asking for. Once the moment has passed, with a child older than three, talk about how you feel when she has a ''hissy fit.'' Remind her, ''We don't always get what we want. You can always ask for what you want, but you won't always get it.'' How many adults keep buying lottery tickets hoping they will win, all the while knowing they won't. All anybody wants is everything, and if you don't ask (or attempt, in some fashion, to get it), you'll never know what things might have come your way. Being an optimist may sometimes bring disappointment, but it can also bring pleasure. Children can use only the tools they have to accomplish their goals.

TELL YOURSELF THAT "TIME TAMES TANTRUMS"

As children grow older, they discover that tantrums and whining are unacceptable methods to win friends and influence people. They change as a matter of survival, and give their parents other behaviors to react to and manage!

BIBLIOTHERAPY

I Was So Mad!, by Norma Simon
Nobody Is Perfick, by Bernard Waber
Sometimes I Like to Cry, by Elizabeth and Harry Stanton
The Temper Tantrum Book, by Edna M. Preston
Throwing Tantrums, by Joy Wilt Berry
Whining, by Joy Wilt Berry

PART THREE

RAISING KIDS
AS A TEAM

BRINGING CHILD-CARE
PROVIDERS AND TEACHERS
ON BOARD

If you and your spouse are going to the trouble of changing your approach to your child, it's important to share your child-raising principles with your child's day-care provider or preschool or kindergarten teacher. The influence and impact of your child's caregiver or teacher must be factored into your overall discipline program. As you make decisions about the type of child care or schooling you will provide for your child and interview providers or teachers, ask pointed and specific questions to see if your child-raising philosophies are compatible. Along with observing with a keen eye the health and safety issues of the day-care or school environment and the degree of stimulation the kids receive, notice if what the child-care provider or teacher says about her approach to discipline jibes with how you see her interacting with the children.

While parents and caregivers or teachers should have similar philosophies about children and discipline, they needn't have identical responses to a child's inappropriate behavior. By its very nature, the caregiver's environment is different from the family home. There are typically a greater number of children who may be of similar or different ages. And there may be a number of adults who work with the kids. Often, the mix of people requires that the discipline policies be more structured than at your home. Day-care providers and teachers know they cannot give in and let infractions slide, because that sets a bad example for the other children and confuses the child who misbehaved. Children need the predictability of the caregiver's responses—which actually provides the child comfort, even when they behaved poorly. While parents should react similarly, they have more attachment to the child, and typically give in more often. Unfortunately, some parents confuse letting the child have his way with a display of love and affection. In reality, constantly acquiescing to a child does him no favors. He learns that pleading, cajoling, and whining will get him what he wants. And that kind of behavior outside of the home can make others want to avoid him, and make friends hard to come by. Kids are too young to know what's best for them. Parents must take a strong and active role in setting parameters and expectations for behavior, right alongside caregivers and teachers.

Here are pointers for how parents and caregivers or teachers can work together to discipline a child in a coordinated way.

VIEW THE PARENT/CHILD-CARE PROVIDER RELATIONSHIP AS A PARTNERSHIP TO ENHANCE THE OVERALL WELL-BEING OF YOUR CHILD

One of the most important factors in the partnership that develops between parents and day-care workers or teachers is open, honest communication. These people will be spending many hours with your child—in some cases more waking hours than you do. You cannot allow this arrangement to flow without discussion between you.

If you approach the relationship from a position of "boss," you will not gain a caregiver's or teacher's support. But if you recognize the value of the relationship as a partnership, your child will be the winner. Working together, dealing with problems, and celebrating the joys of developmental milestones enhance your relationship with your child's caregiver and helps you have an added partner watching out for your child's well-being.

SET REGULAR MEETINGS
If the facility doesn't arrange for regular update meetings, arrange them yourself. Discussing, with ego in check, issues that concern you can provide a wealth of support and resources you may not be aware of or have access to.

SHARE YOUR CONCERNS WITH CAREGIVERS OR TEACHERS
When you have concerns about the care your child is receiving, bring them to the attention of those involved. Very often the problem is more a matter of misunderstanding than anything else. If no communication is initiated, the problem can become the proverbial "mountain out of a molehill." If you don't open the door for discussion, you don't give anyone the opportunity to correct a situation or at least explain the problem from his or her perspective.

VISIT OR WORK IN YOUR CHILD'S CLASS
Try to schedule some time when you can visit the center or school and participate in some of the activities with your child and her friends. (Usually the adults in charge are grateful for parental involvement.) While your child

may act differently when you're around, you'll still get a good sense of how she behaves outside your home. It will also let you see how the caregiver or teacher interacts with different types of children.

ASK QUESTIONS OR RAISE CONCERNS WITHOUT SECOND-GUESSING

Certainly conflicts will arise in the relationship between you and the caregiver or teacher. Parents want their child to receive one-on-one care, while a caregiver may have six or twelve children in her group all wanting that extra something. It can't be done. Children's misdoings occur in the best of circumstances, and caregivers and teachers cannot be expected to control every aspect of your children's behavior. If you have questions or concerns, raise them. Don't assume anything. But approach them from a position of inquiry and not accusation.

UNDERSTAND HOW KIDS REACT IN LARGE GROUPS

In a large group setting, children will misbehave not only for all of the reasons already addressed in this book, but also because of the nature of the environment. Sharing the attention of one or a few adults among many children isn't easy. Some children will establish their independence early and be fine in this kind of environment. Other children will struggle or be seen as problematic because of their personalities and temperaments.

WORK AS A TEAM TO SET BEHAVIOR PARAMETERS

Caregivers and teachers are far more willing to help children achieve better self-control and more likely to succeed if they feel the parents are interested and willing to work with them. It's reasonable to expect that when your child is in the care of others, the caregiver or teacher will take the responsibility of dealing with the daily misbehaviors and not bring them to you to "fix." However, if the caregiver asks for your assistance in what appears to be a chronic problem, presenting a united front to your child is very often the necessary ingredient for change.

Sometimes children are confused about who's in charge, and they'll test the boundaries to force someone to take control. If neither parent nor caretaker accepts the challenge, or if one does and the other doesn't demonstrate support, the child will seize the opportunity to control matters himself—or divide and conquer. Instead, the child should receive the same message from parent and caregiver. That way, the child gets the message that this behavior will not be tolerated. Additionally, if the behavior in question is one exhibited at home as well as at child care or school, the provider or teacher and parent can agree on a similar consequence. This ensures that your child gets the message that these behaviors are unacceptable—in any setting. In some instances, this joint effort will require a great deal of time and energy. Some children just push the envelope as far as it will go and then some. But the partnership will provide the strength that couldn't be achieved singularly by either party.

DETERMINE WHO WILL INVOKE CONSEQUENCES FOR MISBEHAVIOR AT DAY CARE OR SCHOOL

It's important there be a clear determination about who shall discipline the child for inappropriate behavior at school. Children should not be disciplined twice for the same infraction. If the child has paid the price of a misdeed at child care or school, the parents' responsibility is to reinforce the rules of the facility and not punish their child again.

TRY NOT TO TAKE YOUR CHILD'S BEHAVIOR AT DAY CARE OR SCHOOL PERSONALLY

If you're asked to attend a meeting to discuss your child's behavior problem, try not to become defensive. Don't think that other people are judging you by your child's behavior. Don't give in to thoughts like "If I were a better parent, my child would not behave this way!" If only it were that simple.

Listen carefully to what is being said. Ask questions. Appreciate the concerns of the teachers or caregivers. Remember, your child is just one of many children. While he may be an angel for you, it may be that he experiences sibling-type stress in large groups (refer to the "Sibling Rivalry" chapter) and behaves very differently in such settings.

GET YOUR CHILD'S VIEWS

If your child is old enough to tell you his side of the issue, bring him into the discussion after you and the caregiver or teacher have met. Ask him how he sees the problem. Of course, his perspective is rather egocentric, but he'll most likely tell you the truth . . . from his perspective. Learning problem-solving skills is an important lesson for children, so ask him how he thinks the problem can be resolved. Don't presuppose that his answer will be worthless. Respect his input even if you don't agree.

TEACH YOUR CHILD TO WORK OUT CONFLICT

Unfortunately, large group settings often cannot accommodate the child who falls outside of the mainstream. Mix into a group one child with a will of her own and an independent spirit, and you'll spark a combustible situation. If you react to conflict at child care or school by immediately removing your child from the environment, you may find that your child doesn't learn how to overcome friction. One of life's valuable lessons comes from seeing something through even though it's difficult. If you keep changing environments because your child says she's not happy, you're not teaching her the skills necessary to live with things she cannot change. As long as the situation doesn't put your child in harm's way, you might consider letting her struggle.

RECOGNIZE WHEN A SITUATION IS TRULY NOT WORKING AND A CHANGE IS IN ORDER

When you and your child have tried repeatedly to make a day-care or school situation work, but to no avail, it may be time to consider a change of environments. Sometimes the chemistry is just not right. This doesn't imply that any party in the relationship is a failure—only that the situation isn't the right one.

LET THE REINFORCEMENTS SHORE YOU UP

Being able to share the jobs and stresses of raising kids with a good caregiver or teacher can making parenting easier. Most child-care providers and teachers are kind and caring people who want to help your child be the best he can be, and offer you the same kind of support. Accept this helping hand graciously, and you'll benefit in ways beyond measure.

MOM AND DAD IN SYNC:

TEN MYTHS TO FORGET
ABOUT PARENTING

One of the biggest conflicts that exist between husbands and wives is how to bring up baby. You and your spouse come to the role of parenting with paradigms based on the child-rearing style and day-to-day dynamics that were used in each of your family's as well as your community's culture. You bring your unique perspective and individual baggage to the family you're raising.

If you were brought up in a home with five siblings, your childhood experiences will be totally different from those of your spouse if he was raised as an only child. Likewise, imagine if you think the way to be a ''good'' parent is to act as a drill sergeant, and your spouse believes that children have an innate sense of what's right and wrong and don't need much parental influence. With these extremes, your family is destined for a guest appearance on television talk shows.

The key to family harmony is a mother and father working together for the benefit of the child. It demands hard work, but it's not an impossible task. It takes honesty, the ability to see things from a different perspective, and the willingness to compromise.

In the blush of a child-free relationship, the conversations between men and women wanting children are more illusory than reality-based. Once that little life enters the picture, harsh reality takes the place of dreams. Parenting is a lot harder than any of us ever imagine. It's not the 2 A.M. feedings or the shuttling to day care. It's not the extra cooking and cleaning that get to us. It's the stuff discipline is made of that spends our emotions and energy faster than any other demand. We quickly learn that though we have designed a physical and emotional environment to allow our child to reach his full potential, our child has his own agenda, wants, and needs.

To get in sync in raising your kids, it's essential to dispel parenting myths that can prevent you from achieving your best.

MYTH ONE

Once you set the plan and goals for raising your child, you must stick to it no matter what

The best way to approach the issue of how to raise your child is first to decide, as a team (Mom and Dad), your goals for your child. If you're both working toward the same end, it will be easier to unite on the issues that arise. While your overall goals and objectives should be able to stand the test of time, your manner of achieving them will change with each child and continue to change as each child proceeds through developmental milestones. The way you interact with a toddler is different from the way you approach a ten-year-old, which is different from the way you discipline a teenager. And what works for your compliant five-year-old may not have any impact at all on your strong-willed three-year-old.

The parent/child relationship cannot be peacefully layed out from start to finish. It's an interactive relation-

ship, and the best-laid plans become awash in the unknown variable of a child's personality and temperament.
You don't know what your child will be like until your
little bundle arrives on the planet. So even with the best
of intentions before a child's arrival, you may have to
radically change your plans afterward.

The most crucial elements to successfully raising a
caring, contributing, responsible, happy child are for
mothers and fathers to do it as a team and to be flexible
to deal with what their youngster lays at their feet. Since
you don't know what type of child you'll be blessed with
or what direction your child's temperament will take as
he grows, it will be in your own best interest to remain
adaptable. Standing rigidly behind a plan of action that's
contrary to the needs of the child will be unsatisfying and
fraught with anger and frustration.

Don't try to predict your child's behavior; stay loose
and ready. Parents will find that even with the best of
plans, they can't predict every occurrence in advance.
All children are different and react to crisis differently.
When necessary, hold mini "summit meetings" between
parents to compare notes and consider alternatives. As
with any "business," when things aren't going as
planned, restrategizing or reorganization may be in
order.

MYTH TWO

Spouses must parent in the same way or they'll confuse the child

Children are flexible and learn early on how to behave in
different environments with different people who make
different demands on them. (That's why your four-year-

old will whine to Mommy but not dare use the same technique to get what she wants from Dad.)

Raising kids as a team doesn't mean you have to be clones and do everything the same. How could you? You're two unique individuals. It does mean adhering to a plan based on solid principles of child rearing that put your child's and your family's welfare first. This kind of united approach keeps your child grounded and you on target. Though times will be tough as you mold your little one and send her on her course to adolescence and adulthood, it will be a lot easier when you have a partner by your side supporting you.

When Mom and Dad consider parenting a shared partnership with equal yet separate relationships with their child, they will both experience the delight and the distress of best- and worst-parent status on their child's "list." Sharing such honors allows each parent to maintain his individuality while participating as a team. Children will recognize the ability of their parents to support each other and yet be separate, and will mirror this attribute to their children.

MYTH THREE

Parents can't have their separate pet peeves

While parents need to allow each other to have their own subjective list of annoying behaviors, they don't have to adopt those annoying manners onto their own list of petty grievances. One parent may think it's cute when their little darling invades their dresser drawer for dress-up clothes. The other parent may abhor anyone rifling through his clothes. Your child is perfectly capable of learning this distinction and respecting each parent's perspective. Parents don't need to make a hard-and-fast rule that says "Children stay out of drawers at all times" just to accommodate one parent. When you understand this, you can relax. It's not contradictory to tell a child, "Your behavior is a problem *for me,* even if it's not a problem for your dad."

MYTH FOUR

Kids can't have different rules for different times and places

In this hustle-bustle world, children are subject to the rules of many different roads, and they organize them quite beautifully. At Grandma's house they know not to run inside or touch Grandma's things. At the home of a friend, they learn that cleanliness and tidiness are the ruling passions, while at their house as long as they clean up their mess, they're allowed temporary mass destruction. Children go to school, child care, Scouts, sports, and homes of friends, family, and strangers. They observe and interpret the rules and can adjust their behavior to accommodate their surroundings.

MYTH FIVE

Parents have to react similarly every time an incident arises

It's not fair for parents to expect themselves always to react in the same way to their children's antics. As a feeling human being with a wide range of emotions, what is a problem for you one day may not bother you at all the next. You don't have to feel guilty if you tell your child that you can't tolerate something at the moment. Your kids' bickering and brawling may be just enough to send you through the roof when you're on the phone. But when you're relaxing out back in the sunshine and you hear their screams, you may enter the fray and offer marshmallows as weapons of combat. Let your kids know what you need from them and why. While consistency is the key to raising kids, there has to be room for flexibility in a parent's tolerance level. Remember, you're only human. But it's your responsibility to alert your kids to your feelings and give them the chance to respond before you blow.

MYTH SIX
You have to treat all of your children the same

As a child begins to express his own unique personality, parents have to develop a "plan of response" to inappropriate behaviors that works for that child's temperament. Don't get caught in the myth that all children have to be dealt with in exactly the same manner. You merely have to look at some children crossly and they shape up. For others, you have to be firm and rigidly consistent to get the same response. Each child has specific needs, and you must rise to the challenge of meeting them.

MYTH SEVEN
Inappropriate behaviors are objective and concrete

Except for a few biggies, most inappropriate behaviors are subjective. They're what the adult can't tolerate, and each adult has a different tolerance level for different things at different times.

The "big" issues include hurting others physically or

emotionally, destroying property, and taking something that doesn't belong to you. In many cases, the rest of the issues are both subjective and minor. They're the little annoyances that sometimes affect you and sometimes don't, depending upon your physical and emotional health at the moment of the annoying behavior.

Decide what major behaviors are intolerable and unacceptable and what consequences will be effective to modify or eliminate them. Consensus on this will help bypass the tried-and-true method of "divide and conquer"—an innate talent children are born with to get parents to do exactly what they want! If Mom and Dad are firm on the issues considered critical to participating joyfully in the human race, children will comply.

MYTH EIGHT
Children shouldn't be included in discipline discussions

When children are around four, start including them in the behavior management/discipline discussion. Family meetings that afford a child a safe place to air her grievances and participate in the family will begin the process of teaching her to be a responsible adult and parent. Set up rules for these gatherings that can be as formal or informal as you want. Some families actually have a president, secretary, and treasurer, and each person (children included) rotates through the positions. Other families have each person write down what he or she wants to talk about at the meeting. Then those papers are drawn from a bowl and discussed, in no predetermined order, so that no one person or issue appears more powerful than the others.

Family meetings must support a policy of common courtesy. Rudeness or disrespect from any member can't be tolerated. If this is to be a place where children learn appropriate ways to resolve problems, allowing a child to call a sibling "dumb head" will not accomplish your goal. If children know there is a safe forum for them to talk about their roles in the family, they will be inclined to tell their parents how they feel.

At these meetings, parents can discuss behavior problems and ask for input from the children to find satisfactory resolutions. Listen carefully to what your children tell you and keep your reactions calm. As the adults and heads of the family by virtue of your age and experience, you have more authority and privilege than they do. But as members of the same family they need to have the right to disagree with you. When children feel they have a say, they're more inclined to work toward the same goals as other family members. And when they understand why or how their behavior affects others, they're on the path to change.

MYTH NINE
A family can't be a democracy

Moms and Dads who maintain a minidemocracy in their families find they spend less time being the disciplinarian and more time enjoying the family. It's possible to set up a menu of consequences and allow children to choose from the menu. Remember, though, that parents don't always behave well, and children will want to see a parent experience the consequences of his or her behavior, too. Parents forget to do their chores (or choose to postpone doing them) and say things for which they are later sorry. If children are required to make amends, so should parents be.

The democratic family allows both parents and children to experience a feeling of power with a spirit of cooperation.

MYTH TEN
Parenting shouldn't be fun

Children will integrate the rules of their family into the fabric of who they are. But the memories they have of childhood will be the fun family get-together times. They'll remember the time Dad took the top off the pressure cooker too soon and "steamed the ceiling," or when Mom tried to surprise Dad by painting the living room bright orange. They'll remember days in the park and family celebrations with joy and pass those memories on to their children.

Take a moment to reflect on your childhood memories. What do you remember? Are they the same type of memories you want your child to have? If so, duplicate the experiences. If not, change them for your child.

Creating pleasurable childhood memories is possible. Sprinkle good times generously throughout your child's life. These will stand up longer to the scrutiny of time than all of the time spent "teaching them a lesson." If you believe "reprimanding and criticizing" are the means to teach your child how to become a successful grown-up, you will see parenting as another "job." You and your child will spend most of your life together locked in an ugly struggle that leaves all parties exhausted, unhappy, and angry. Which memories of childhood do you want your child to have?

When you take delight in your child's accomplishments and share as many glorious moments with your child as possible, the times when you had to "pull rank" will be just minor memories.

There is so much parents can learn from their children. Children experience every new event with the joy and excitement of opening up a beautifully wrapped gift. They celebrate life and enjoy all it has to offer. Allow yourself to join them for the ride of a lifetime; you'll remember the joys of your childhood and share the joys of theirs.

Parenting is hard work, but if you take it so seriously that you forget to appreciate the main characters (you and your children), the play will be over one day and you'll have little to savor.

Take time to enjoy your child. If you spend too much time "raising" him, you'll miss out on all the fun things kids do while growing up. Don't let your child grow up and move out and then wish you'd done things differently or made more time for him. Save anger and discipline for the really necessary occasions, and let other indiscretions pass. Remember, to change your child's behavior, you have to change yours first. If you have fun parenting, chances are your kids will be a pleasure to parent!

INDEX

Abandonment fears, 74–76, 79
Abuse, physical, 82
Acting-out behavior, 88–97
  alternatives to, 92–93
  anger and, 91–92, 94–95
  for attention, 92–93, 97
  influences on, 93–94, 96
Age-appropriate behavior, 13–26
  examples/approaches to, 23–26
  expectations/consequences for, 20–22
  parental perspectives, 14–18, 109–10
  when to correct, 18–20
  See also specific behavior
Anger
  child's expression of, 90, 91, 94–95, 167, 170–71
  child's independence and, 102–3
  child's reaction to, 13–14
  about lying, 111
  parents' expression of, 172
  parents' time-out from, 105
  while shopping, 131
Apologies, 115–16
Attention-getting. *See specific behavior*

Baby, new, 146–51
Bedtime behavior, 29–41
  child sleeping with parents, 36–37
  delay tactics, 34–35

and morning routine effects, 38–41
  nighttime fears and, 37
  sleep-time and, 35–36
  stress-relieving routines, 31–38
  transition time and, 33–34
Bibliotherapy
  acting out, 97
  bedtime, 41
  dressing, 50
  following instructions, 74
  going places, 87
  independence, 106
  lying, 119
  manners, 128
  mealtime, 63
  passive behavior, 162
  shopping, 137
  sibling rivalry/new baby, 151
  tantrums and whining, 173
Birth-order dynamics, 141–42
Biting, 88–97
Body language, 89, 111
Books and reading, 29–30, 33, 107–8, 113, 147; *See also* Bibliotherapy

CHILD acronym, 23
Clean-up chores, 69, 72–74
Community programs, 160
Compromise techniques, 105–6
Computer games, 159
Conflict. *See* Problem-solving skills

195